Joseph Rhymer

THE ILLUSTRATED
LIFE OF JESUS CHRIST

VIKING

This book is dedicated to Ruth and Anthony Humphreys.

VIKING

Published by the Penguin Group

Penguin Books Canada Ltd, 10 Alcorn Avenue, Toronto, Ontario, Canada, M4V 3B2

Penguin Books Ltd, 27 Wrights Lane, London W8 5TZ, England

Viking Penguin, a division of Penguin Books USA Inc., 375 Hudson Street. New York, New York 10014, USA

Penguin Books Australia Ltd, Ringwood, Victoria, Australia

Penguin Books (NZ) Ltd, 182-190 Wairau Road, Auckland 10, New Zealand

Penguin Books Ltd, Registered Offices: Harmondsworth, Middlesex, England

First published 1991

1 3 5 7 9 10 8 6 4 2

Canadian Cataloguing in Publication Data

Rhymer, Joseph, 1927 –
The illustrated life of Christ

ISBN 0-670-84137-4

1. Jesus Christ – Biography. I. Title.

BT301.2.R48 1991   232.9'01   C91-093641-2

Design styling by Marnie Searchwell
Layout design by Michael Gowdy
Picture researcher: Anne-Marie Ehrlich
Project editor: Kate Newman
Typeset by James Lee
Printed and bound in China

CONTENTS

INTRODUCTION

The four books of the New Testament called 'gospels' only make full sense if the many stories and incidents in them are related to the central theme: who Jesus was, what he achieved, and how this affected everyday life. A modern reader does not have to accept the beliefs of the first Christians, but without some awareness of what they did believe about Jesus of Nazareth much of the gospel material will seem incomprehensible, or at best a mere collection of legends.

The gospel stories about Jesus were first told after his death in the public sermons given by the disciples who had been with him during his brief ministry. These men illustrated their teaching about Jesus with incidents from his life, and the stories were also used during the private weekly meetings for 'the breaking of bread' (the Lord's Supper), to help the worshippers to understand why they were meeting and what they were doing. The four gospels are collections of these stories about Jesus, organized round a set of beliefs and given a chronological framework.

The first Christians believed that Jesus had brought in a new age for the whole world by his life, death and resurrection, and that he reigns at the right hand of God as Lord of the Universe; that Jesus had sent the Holy Spirit as the sign of his risen power and glory; that this new age would shortly reach its climax with the return of Jesus, appointed by

God to be judge both of the living and of the dead; and that anyone could share in the benefits of this new age by believing in Jesus, repenting and accepting baptism, when they would receive the Holy Spirit and be forgiven their sins.

Such beliefs were supported by drawing on Messianic prophecies in the Old Testament as references to Jesus. These included the promises made by God first to Abraham, Isaac, Jacob, and later to all the Hebrew people at the Exodus from Egypt. Jesus was the new King David, who was also born in Bethlehem. References to a servant of God whose sufferings brought forgiveness to others were applied to Jesus. He was also the mysterious 'Son of Man' who would come to earth as judge riding on the clouds.

The stories about Jesus and the reports of what he had said were recounted to support these beliefs. Only later were the separate items woven together into the four gospels we now have – Matthew, Mark, Luke and John. Most scholars believe that at least 30 years elapsed after the death of Jesus before the first of these four gospels was compiled, and it may have been as long as 70 years before all four were complete.

From internal evidence, it appears that the four gospels were edited for groups with different backgrounds and needs: Matthew for Jewish Christians in Palestine; Mark for Christians in Rome; Luke for non-Jewish Greek-speaking Christians in the eastern Mediterranean, where Paul had travelled; John for Jewish Christians outside Palestine who needed to defend their beliefs against other religions popular in their region. To compile a 'life of Christ', such as this book, from these four accounts entails ignoring differences between the gospels, with the inevitable risk of omission and distortion. The text used for quotations is the King James 'Authorized' Version.

The life of Jesus has been one of the main inspirations for western art, and artists have frequently expressed his significance for their own times and situations by depicting the events of the gospels in their own surroundings. Not only have they shown Jesus against the background of their own familiar localities, they have sometimes incorporated their patrons, their contemporaries and themselves in the scenes they have depicted. Consequently, the people of the artists' own times and backgrounds would readily perceive a wealth of meaning and symbolism in the incidents depicted. The illustrations have been chosen to show how art can be used to express the significance of Jesus for times, places and cultures very different from the Palestine of his own day.

THE ANNUNCIATION

And in the sixth month the angel Gabriel was sent from God
unto a city of Galilee, named Nazareth, to a virgin espoused to
a man whose name was Joseph, of the house of David; and the
virgin's name was Mary.

Luke 1:26-27

Only two of the four gospels, Matthew and Luke, have accounts of the
birth and infancy of Jesus, and each approaches the story in a different
way, to serve the needs of their different readerships. Matthew's
Gospel was compiled for Palestinian Jews who had become Christians; Luke's Gospel
was aimed at the more cosmopolitan Greek-speaking world of the eastern
Mediterranean.

Luke's Gospel emphasizes the role played by women, so he tells the story through
Mary's eyes. In Luke's account, the angel Gabriel appeared to Mary in her home in
Nazareth and told her that she was highly favoured because the Lord was with her. She
was to bear a son, the angel continued, who would be called 'Son of the Highest'. He
would be given 'the throne of his father David' to reign over a kingdom without end.

Naturally, Mary was bewildered, for marital relations were not permitted before the
end of a year's betrothal, and she was still a virgin. It was then that the angel revealed
that this would not be a normal conception; the child would be conceived by the Holy
Spirit, and this was why 'that holy thing which shall be born of thee shall be called the
Son of God'.

Gabriel went on to tell Mary that her cousin Elizabeth, who lived down in Judaea

1

4

And the angel came in unto her, and said, Hail, thou that art highly favoured, the Lord is with thee: blessed art thou among women.

Luke 1:28

The Annunciation
Sandro Botticelli (1445–1510),
Uffizi Gallery, Florence.

Painted *c*1488 for the convent of Castello just outside Florence, Botticelli adapted a design by Donatello and included a view of the local landscape. The angel is telling Mary that she has been chosen by God to be the mother of Jesus.

and was well on in years, had also conceived and was six months pregnant. Her child would be John the Baptist, who would prepare the ground for Jesus's preaching.

Mary accepted the extraordinary situation, and by her willing consent expressed the element of human cooperation which marked all the covenants made by God: 'Behold the handmaid of the Lord; be it unto me according to thy word.'

As a Jew writing for thoroughly patriarchal Jews, Matthew tells the story from Joseph's point of view: Joseph and Mary were only betrothed to each other and not yet married, but betrothal created obligations which were almost as binding as marriage. With Mary pregnant, and knowing that the child would not be his, Joseph planned quietly to end the betrothal, perhaps to save his own face, but mainly to spare Mary ostracism by the local community. If they had been married, Mary would have committed adultery, for which the legal penalty was death.

Again, an angel intervened, this time in a dream to Joseph to explain that Mary was pregnant by the Holy Spirit. A well-known prophecy by Isaiah lent credibility to the angel's explanation, for Isaiah had said that a virgin would conceive a son who would be named Immanuel, which means 'God is with us'.

Joseph, like Mary, freely accepted the divine plan, and married his pregnant Mary. At worst, the local community would only assume that he and Mary had broken the conventions of betrothal.

Like most prophecies, the original passage in Isaiah had an immediate significance for Isaiah's own times. The child Immanuel was a sign of approaching catastrophe, to warn Isaiah's king that he has made a political decision which would bring disaster on his people. In this case, God's presence would bring punishment, not protection, because the king had betrayed God's trust in him. Matthew's Jewish-Christian readers would be familiar with the passage, and the warning would not be lost on them. The birth of Jesus was not itself a guarantee of security; favour in God's sight required unconditional trust in God.

Now the birth of Jesus Christ was on this wise: When as his mother Mary was espoused to Joseph, before they came together, she was found with child of the Holy Ghost. Then Joseph her husband, being a just man and not willing to make her a publick example, was minded to put her away privily.

Matt 1:18-19

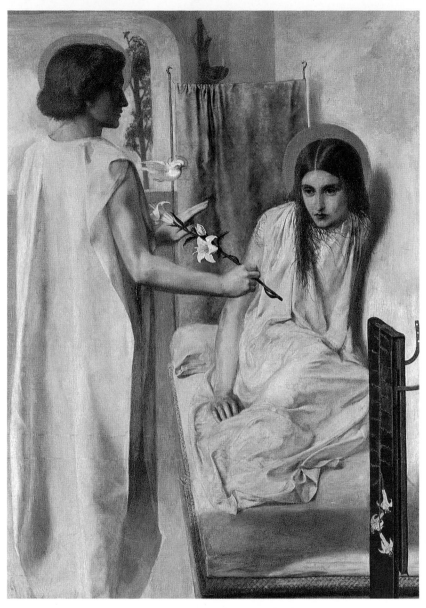

The Annunciation
Dante Gabriel Rossetti
(1828–1882), Tate Gallery,
London.

And, behold, thou
shalt conceive in
thy womb, and
bring forth a son,
and call his name
Jesus.

Luke 1:31

Painted in 1850, Rossetti intended it to be part of a diptych with the
death of Mary, but he never started the other painting. The angel bears a
lily, the symbol of innocence, as he tells Mary that she is to be the mother
of Jesus.

The Annunciation
Leonardo da Vinci (1452–1519),
Uffizi Gallery, Florence.

Possibly painted *c*1472, soon after Leonardo became a member of the painters' guild in Florence and while he was still a pupil of Verrocchio. Set in an imaginary landscape with a busy river, Italian trees and a lush carpet of flowers, it emphasizes the mystery and the relevance of the angel's message to Mary.

THE VISITATION AND
THE BIRTH OF JOHN
THE BAPTIST

My soul doth magnify the Lord, and my spirit hath rejoiced in God my saviour. For he hath regarded the low estate of his handmaiden: for, behold, from henceforth all generations shall call me blessed.

Luke 1:46-48

Immediately after the annunciation to Mary, Luke records a visit by Mary to her cousin Elizabeth, who lived with her husband Zechariah near Jerusalem. Zechariah was a Hebrew priest, one of the many who did a spell of duty in the Temple in Jerusalem officiating at the daily sacrifices. Some months earlier, while tending the incense brazier in the Temple, an angel had told him that his wife would bear a son by him, who would be the herald of the Messiah.

Zechariah had protested that both he and his wife were past the age where they could expect to have children, but the angel had insisted on the truth of his message and had struck Zechariah dumb for his scepticism. The boy was to be John the Baptist, due to be born shortly before Jesus. The incident had strong echoes of the birth of Isaac to the elderly Abraham and Sarah, of Jacob and Esau to Isaac and the barren Rebecca, and of Samuel to Hannah (Gen 18:9ff; 25:20ff; 1 Sam 1:4ff), but although the conception of John the Baptist was in the face of natural expectations, there was no question of this being another virgin birth.

When Mary, pregnant with Jesus, arrived in Elizabeth's house and greeted her, the future John the Baptist leapt in Elizabeth's womb. Elizabeth herself was filled with the

The Visitation
Domenico Ghirlandaio
(1449–1494), Church of Santa
Maria Novella, Florence.

One of the great series of frescos of the lives of the Virgin Mary and John
the Baptist commissioned for Santa Maria Novella in 1485. In a Florentine
setting, it depicts Mary, pregnant with Jesus, visiting her cousin
Elizabeth, pregnant with John the Baptist.

Holy Spirit, and greeted Mary as particularly blessed among women, both for the child she was bearing and for her act of faith. Elizabeth's greeting complemented the message given to Mary by the angel Gabriel, and acknowledged the supreme importance of Mary's willing acceptance of her role in God's plan.

In response, Mary introduced a favourite theme of Luke's Gospel; that God comes to the help of the poor and the simple, and works through them, rather than through the rich. The poem Mary spoke, known as the 'Magnificat' from the opening word of the Latin translation, has become one of the best known and loved in the Bible: 'My soul doth magnify the Lord ...' It tells of the mercy and strength of God, who scatters the proud and exalts the lowly, fills the hungry and sends the rich away empty. The Magnificat is rich in quotations from a wide range of passages in the Hebrew scriptures, but mostly it echoes the Song of Hannah, mother of the prophet Samuel, whose prayer for a child was answered by God. Hannah's song of joy exalted God as the saviour of the poor.

Luke's account of the birth and childhood of Jesus compares it with the birth and childhood of John the Baptist, who would preach repentance and prepare the Jews of Palestine for the coming of Jesus as Messiah. For both children, there were overtones of the 'Nazirite' vow, by which a boy such as Samuel was formally dedicated to God for a period or for life. Matthew needs only to refer to the Nazirite vow by name for his Jewish readers, linking it by sound with Jesus's home town of Nazareth (Matt 2:23). Luke needs to be more explicit for non-Jewish readers in his report of the conception of John the Baptist: 'For he shall be great in the sight of the Lord, and shall drink neither wine nor strong drink.'

> Now Elizabeth's full time came that she should be delivered; and she brought forth a son.
>
> Luke 1:57

John the Baptist was duly born, and was circumcised on the eighth day. John's father was released from his dumbness after he had signalled for writing materials and he gave his child the name commanded by the angel. Zechariah immediately spoke the great poem explaining the significance of his son's birth, familiar to us from the opening word of its Latin translation, 'Benedictus': 'Blessed be the Lord God of Israel; for he hath visited and redeemed his people ...' Once more, the long poem is rich with quotations from psalms and the prophetic writings, to emphasize that the births expected in these two unimportant families were the culmination of all that God had promised to the Hebrew people.

At an undisclosed time before Jesus began his public ministry, John went to live in the desolate region where the River Jordan winds down to the Dead Sea and the Essenes of Qumran had their monastery. His mission of preaching repentance would reach its climax with the baptism of Jesus.

The Birth of John the Baptist
12th-century fresco in the Chapel
of St. Gabriel, crypt of Canterbury
Cathedral.

The building represents the Temple in Jerusalem in the idiom of Norman
architecture. John the Baptist's father, struck dumb for doubting that he
and his elderly wife could have a child, is holding a vellum strip with
John's name written on it.

13

THE BIRTH OF JESUS

And Joseph also went up from Galilee, out of the city of
Nazareth, into Judaea, unto the city of David, which is called
Bethlehem; (because he was of the house and lineage of David):
To be taxed with Mary his espoused wife, being great with child.

Luke 2:4-5

As Luke was writing a systematic account for a distinguished official, Theophilus, and for a cosmopolitan readership, he took care to relate the birth of Jesus to an official act of the Roman Empire. This consisted of a census held during Quirinius's first term as governor of the Roman province of Syria (which included Palestine), while Herod the Great still reigned as the local king appointed by the Romans.

All householders had to return to their tribal centre or birthplace, so Joseph and Mary travelled the 90 miles from Nazareth to Bethlehem, four miles south of Jerusalem, which was the official centre for the Hebrew tribe of Judah. There is no mention of Nazareth in the Old Testament, but Bethlehem was an ancient centre which had been the birthplace of King David, from whom Joseph was descended. There are records of a similar census in the Roman province of Egypt for which all were required to return to their home towns.

The Virgin and Child in Glory
Sandro Botticelli (1445-1510),
Uffizi Gallery, Florence (right).

Commissioned by the Arte della
Seta of Florence in 1488,
Botticelli completed this
magnificent altarpiece in 1490. It
shows Mary holding Jesus while
gazing indulgently at him
blessing the viewer. Mother and
child are framed by a background
of angels dancing and singing.

The Virgin of Autun
(The Madonna of Chancellor Rolin)
by Jan van Eyck (c1385–1441),
Louvre, Paris.

Commissioned by Rolin, Chancellor of Burgundy, van Eyck painted it
c1435. It depicts Rolin kneeling before the glorified Mary and Jesus,
almost as an equal, with Autun, the residence of the dukes of Burgundy, in
the background.

La Notte
(Scene of the Nativity)
Correggio (c1489–1534)
Gemaldegalerie, Dresden.

Finished *c*1530, Correggio depicts the newly-born Jesus in Mary's arms against a background of the first light of dawn. The glory of the divine child provides the illumination to reveal the contrast between the amazed peasants and the adoring angels.

17

The Nativity
Giotto di Bondone (*c*1267-1337),
Scrovegni Chapel, Padua.

Born near Florence, Giotto is
claimed as the founder of Italian
Renaissance painting. His fresco
depicting the birth of Jesus is part
of the great series commissioned
by Enrico Scrovegni in 1306 for
the chapel he built in Padua in
honour of the Virgin of the
Annunciation.

There in Bethlehem 'the days were accomplished' and Jesus was born. It is a favourite phrase of Luke's, and he uses it to indicate that the ancient promises made by God had been fulfilled. More significant still is the word translated as 'firstborn', for in Hebrew history the patriarchal blessings and the covenants had been transmitted through the firstborn, so the term also had Messianic overtones.

Tradition has located the birth in a cave, now beneath the great Christian basilica of the Nativity founded early in the 4th century by Helena, the mother of the Roman Emperor Constantine. This is consistent with the practice of using caves as dwellings, as well as shelter for animals, sometimes with a large porch added to provide extra accommodation. The word translated as 'inn' may convey too grand an idea, for it could just refer to such a porch built to provide extra accommodation.

Matthew gives no details of the birth of Jesus, but emphasizes his divine parentage by stressing that Joseph had no marital relations with Mary before Jesus was born. Nor, for that matter, does Matthew's account imply that they had marital relations afterwards. The gospel accounts do not make it clear whether Mary had any more children after Jesus.

18

The Madonna Nursing the Child,
with Greyhounds and a Peacock in a
Garden
The Master of the Embroidered
Leaf; private collection.

The anonymous, early-16th-century painter gets his title from the
beautiful detail of magnificently embroidered leaves on Mary's robe and on
the tapestry behind her throne. She is shown suckling the infant Jesus.

THE ADORATION BY
THE SHEPHERDS

And there were in the same country shepherds abiding in the field, keeping watch over their flock by night. And, lo, the angel of the Lord came upon them, and the glory of the Lord shone round about them: and they were sore afraid.

Luke 2:8-9

In its account of the angel and the shepherds, Luke's Gospel continues the theme of God's special concern for the poor, already expressed so strongly in the Magnificat (Luke 1:46-55), and implicit in the choice of Zechariah and Elizabeth, and Joseph and Mary for such grave responsibilities. Matthew highlights the event with the arrival of wise men bearing precious gifts, but Luke gives the reaction of some of the most deprived people of Bethlehem to the news of the birth of Jesus.

The birth was first announced during the night by an angel, to shepherds guarding their sheep on the outskirts of Bethlehem. The angel calmed their fears and reminded them that Bethlehem was the city of David. Then he told them that the Saviour-Messiah of Hebrew tradition had been born there, and he gave them precise details of where they could find the child. Suddenly, the angel was surrounded by a crowd of angels singing of God's glory and the consequences of the event for peace and good will on earth.

The shepherds hastened to the scene of the birth, and when they had seen Mary, Joseph and the infant Jesus they went away to spread the news of what had happened and what had been revealed to them about its significance.

Shepherds might represent very different levels in Hebrew society. They could be the

And the angel said
unto them, Fear
not; for, behold, I
bring you good
tidings of great joy,
which shall be to
all people. For
unto you is born
this day in the city
of David a
Saviour, which is
Christ the Lord.

Luke 2:10-11

Adoration of the Shepherds
From the Hours of Bonaparte
Chislieri, British Library, London.

Books of 'hours' contained the readings for the daily religious services
required of the clergy but also said by devout lay people. The child Jesus is
being adored by the shepherds in an idyllic pastoral setting. The Magi are
just coming into view.

poorest of labourers, only a stage better than destitute, who lived in conditions little better than the sheep they guarded from predators and theft. On the other hand, the Hebrews proudly traced their ancestry from such nomadic shepherds as Abraham, Isaac and Jacob, with whom God made the first covenants and established the Israelites as his chosen people.

Traditions and laws from the times of the patriarchal shepherds still exercised a powerful influence on the Hebrews long after they had become a settled, agricultural society with kings and all the apparatus of central government. The title 'shepherd' was frequently accorded to God, as in the 23rd Psalm, 'The Lord is my shepherd'. The rulers were expected to be good 'shepherds' of their people, and were condemned as 'bad shepherds' when they failed in their duty.

Passover, the main Hebrew religious feast which commemorated the escape from Egypt (transformed by Christians into Easter), was a shepherds' festival which featured the sacrifice of a lamb for a sacred meal. Throughout the year in the Temple in Jerusalem, sheep were sacrificed twice daily in a ritual expressing God's continuing presence among his people. Jesus referred to himself as 'the good shepherd: the good shepherd giveth his life for the sheep', in a way which united the ideas of shepherd and sacrifice. The story of the shepherds and their adoration of the newly-born Jesus would have had overtones of divine leadership and sacrifice for the first Christians, as well as the obvious theme of God revealing himself first to the poor.

The Adoration of the Shepherds
Stained glass window in the Church of Notre Dame du Cran.

In this triple window the shepherds are bearing simple gifts to the newly-born Jesus, including a basket of eggs, while various saints also join in their adoration.

The phrase 'the glory of the Lord' signified the presence of God himself as redeemer and lawgiver. The glory of the Lord appeared to the Israelites immediately after the crossing of the Red Sea and, above all, it descended on Mount Sinai when God summoned Moses to receive the law. When God ordered Moses and the Israelites to begin the journey from Mount Sinai to the promised land, Moses asked God to reveal his glory as reassurance that he would be present with them.

When the glory of the Lord shone all round the shepherds, they would recognize the experience as the presence of God himself, in a form familiar to them from the descriptions given in the most sacred parts of Hebrew tradition. But while Moses had been unable to go near the tabernacle, the tent which housed the Ark of the Covenant, while the divine power filled it, the shepherds found no difficulty in approaching Mary, Joseph and the infant Jesus, and worshipping the divine presence in the familiar form of a child.

The account of the revelation to the shepherds uses four of the Messianic titles from the old Hebrew promises and predictions: David, Saviour, Christ and Lord. David was the archetypal leader; Saviour echoes the delivery of the Israelites from Egyptian slavery and their journey to the promised land led by Moses; Christ is the Greek word for Messiah, the final deliverer who comes with authority conferred by God; and Lord is the title the Hebrews used instead of 'Yahweh', the personal name of God, which was too sacred to be spoken aloud. The ancient promises all met and were fulfilled in Bethlehem, in the person of Jesus.

The Shepherds said one to another, Let us now go even unto
Bethlehem, and see this thing which is come to pass, which the
Lord hath made known unto us.
And they came with haste, and found Mary, and Joseph, and the
babe lying in a manger.

Luke 2: 15-16

23

THE ADORATION BY THE MAGI

Now when Jesus was born in Bethlehem of Judaea in the days of Herod the king, behold, there came wise men from the east to Jerusalem, saying, Where is he that is born King of the Jews? for we have seen his star in the east, and are come to worship him.

Matt 2:1-2

Matthew approaches the birth of Jesus from another angle. Luke describes the event through the eyes of the poor; Matthew presents the other extreme. He has already established the miraculous, divine conception of Jesus. Now he describes the adoration of the newly-born child by a group who represented learning, wealth and power, 'wise men from the east'.

Popular Christian tradition has designated them kings, but Matthew – writing in Greek – uses the word 'magoi' (Latin 'magi'). Strictly speaking, this means that they were Persian priest-astrologers, but the word was also used to designate astrologers who could interpret dreams and omens, who possessed secret knowledge and understood the mysteries of religion. Matthew does not say that there were three of them.

Adoration of the Magi (detail)
Gentile da Fabriano
(c1370–1427), Uffizi Gallery,
Florence.

Commissioned for the Church of Santa Trinita, Florence, by Palla Strozzi rival of the notorious Cosimo de' Medici, it was completed in 1423. This detail of one side of the painting contains portraits of contemporary citizens of Florence as the retinue of the Magi, a frequent requirement of patrons.

The mention of King Herod is important for locating the birth of Jesus within the chronology of his times, for there is reliable evidence that Herod died in 4BC, so Jesus was born shortly before that date. The 'Christian' system of reckoning years as 'Before Christ' or after Christ – 'Anno Domini' – was not introduced until the 6th century of the Christian era, when an error in reconciling the new system with the Roman method of dating years resulted in the paradox of Jesus being born some years 'BC'.

There has been much speculation about the star, mentioned only by Matthew, which guided the wise men and 'stood over where the young child was', but none of it is conclusive. If it was Halley's Comet, as some have suggested, it would mean dating the birth of Jesus at 11BC, which would place it too long before the death of Herod. A supernova was recorded by Chinese astronomers around the right date, and this would have been unusual enough to be treated as a God-given sign by professional astronomers.

More to the point for Matthew and his Jewish readers, a mysterious prophecy in the ancient Hebrew story of Balaam contains the passage, 'He hath said, which heard the words of God, and knew the knowledge of the Most High [one of the Hebrew titles of God], which saw the vision of the Almighty ... I shall see him but not now: I shall behold him, but not nigh: there shall come a star out of Jacob, and a Sceptre out of Israel ...' (Num 24:16f). This prophecy occurs at a particularly significant moment in Hebrew history, as the Israelites drew near to the promised land on their journey through the wilderness from Egypt. According to the prophecy, this Messianic, star-heralded king of the future will defeat all Israel's enemies. In traditional Hebrew teaching it was thought to refer to King David, but Christians naturally applied it to Jesus, the Messianic 'Son of David'.

Assuming that a king's son would be born in the country's capital city, the wise men went first to King Herod in Jerusalem, to ask where the infant King of the Jews was to be found. Herod consulted the Jewish religious leaders and specialists in the Hebrew sacred writings to ask where the Messiah would be born. They were in no doubt, for there were prophecies both in Micah and in the Hebrew historical records of King David that he would be born in David's native town, Bethlehem. Matthew conflates texts from Micah and 2 Samuel, which predict that Bethlehem would produce a ruler of God's people. Herod sent the wise men to Bethlehem and asked them to return to him so that 'I may come and worship him'.

The gospel only hints at the notorious and murderous reputation of Herod (see 'The Slaughter of the Innocents') in the account of the visit of the wise men, but Matthew records that after Bethlehem they avoided Jerusalem and Herod on their return journey.

The wise men's visit to Jesus signified the homage appropriate to the child who fulfilled Hebrew hopes for a king like David. The rule of the Davidic kings had ended abruptly nearly 600 years earlier when the Babylonians destroyed Jerusalem and exiled its people. When the exiles returned 50 years later they established a society ruled by high priests, and the Davidic monarchy was never restored. The Hebrews retained a deep nostalgia for the period of the Davidic kings, which became the model for their

The Adoration of the Magi
Pieter Brueghel the Elder
(c1525–1569), Civici Musei
Venezia d'Arte e di Storia.

Typically, Brueghel sets the birthplace of Jesus in a corner of an obscure
Flemish village with a ruined church. The visit of the 'wise men' bringing
gifts to the infant Jesus is passing unnoticed by the busy peasants.

Messianic expectations. The gift of gold by the wise men traditionally acknowledged
that Jesus was a king.

Incense – 'frankincense' – in Matthew's account, played an important part in Hebrew
worship, as indeed it still does in many religions. Its main ingredient is a resin from
species of trees found in semi-desert areas, which produces smoke with a strong,
characteristic smell when burned. The Hebrews burned it as a sacrifice on its own special
altar in the Temple. It also figured in the other sacrifices in Hebrew worship and could
only be offered by priests; consequently it represented all priestly responsibilities and
privileges. Offered to the infant Jesus, it symbolized his priestly role.

Myrrh is another resin, from shrubs native to southern Arabia and eastern Africa, and

The Magi Asleep
Stained glass in Canterbury
Cathedral (right).

In this enchanting little scene the
three 'kings' are all asleep in a
bed, wearing their crowns. The
angel represents the dream in
which they were warned not to
return to King Herod to tell him
where the infant Jesus could be
found.

The Adoration of the Magi
Lorenzo Monaco (*c*1370–*c*1425),
Uffizi, Florence (far right).

Painted in Florence shortly after
1423. The opulence and racial
variety of the figures contrast
strongly with the almost abstract
setting. The kings' crowns are
symbolically placed on the ground
as they worship the infant Jesus.

was an ingredient in the special oils used by the Hebrews in the rites for consecrating
the altars, sacred vessels and the priests who used them. It was also used as a painkiller
and for embalming the dead; myrrh occurs again in the gospel story as a drug offered to
Jesus during his crucifixion, and to embalm his body for burial. In the gift of myrrh by
the wise men all of these various usages became symbols of the priestly role of Jesus and
of what he would experience.

Although Matthew's Gospel is written for Christians from a Jewish background, the
visit of the wise men also symbolized the relevance of the birth of Jesus to the wider,
non-Jewish world. This theme is important in all four gospels, and Matthew is no
exception.

When they had heard the king,
they departed; and, lo, the star, which they saw in the east,
went before them,
till it came and stood over where the young child was.

Matthew 2:9

THE PRESENTATION IN THE TEMPLE

A light to lighten the Gentiles, and the glory of thy people Israel.

Luke 2:32

In accordance with Hebrew law, Jesus was circumcised on the eighth day after his birth (Luke 2:12). Whatever may have been the ancient origins of this religious rite, for Hebrews it was an essential sign of the covenant with God, and of the great escape from Egypt. No male could take part in the Passover unless he was circumcised (Ex 12:47-49). Jesus was also named at this ceremony, as was the custom, and given the name Yehosua, the Hebrew word for 'God is saviour', which has come down to us as 'Jesus' through the Greek form of the Aramaic contraction Yesu. ('Christ' is a title rather than a proper name.) By his circumcision Jesus was made a formal member of the people of the covenant, and conformed to Hebrew religious law.

By the same code of law, the mother of a boy was ritually unclean for seven days after the birth (Lev 12:2ff). Consequently, Mary and Joseph went to the Temple in Jerusalem to offer the sacrifice prescribed by the law to render the mother ritually clean again: a lamb, or two pigeons if the people were too poor to afford a lamb.

The occasion was full of significance for the early Christians, for it was the first time that Jesus had entered the Temple which they believed he eventually replaced as the centre of sacrificial worship. Among the throng in the Temple courtyards was a man named Simeon, who spent much of his time there anticipating the final fulfilment of God's promises to his chosen people. Simeon recognized this fulfilment in the infant Jesus, and spoke the poem we now know as the 'Nunc Dimittis', from its opening words in the Latin translation, 'Lord, now lettest thou thy servant depart in peace ...'

The Presentation in the Temple
The Master of St. Severin, Victoria
and Albert Museum, London.

This 16th-century German
stained-glass window from the
Cistercian Abbey of Mariawald in
Eifel gives the incident a 16th
century German Christian setting
at the high altar of a church with
clergy and candle-bearers in
Christian vestments and onlookers
in contemporary German dress.

This poem draws heavily on the four 'Songs of the Servant' in the later chapters of the Book of the Prophet Isaiah. In these poems, God chose an unnamed servant to be the living embodiment of the ancient promises God made to his chosen people, the Hebrews; he would also bring true justice to all nations, give sight to the blind and free the imprisoned. In the course of fulfilling this task, say the poems, the servant would be tortured and killed, but in the end he would be vindicated and rewarded by God. Simeon saw that these prophetic poems were to be fulfilled in Jesus.

THE FLIGHT INTO EGYPT

Behold, the angel of the Lord appeared to Joseph in a dream, saying, Arise, and take the young child and his mother, and flee into Egypt, and be thou there until I bring thee word: for Herod will seek the young child to destroy him.

Matt 2:13

When the magi failed to report back to King Herod, the very poverty of Joseph and Mary saved both them and the infant Jesus. They were too insignificant to attract unwelcome attention when Herod ordered a search for the child he feared might replace him as King of the Jews. The holy family fled to Egypt, possibly to the great city of Alexandria.

Alexandria, on the Mediterranean coast of Egypt, had been founded in 332BC by Alexander the Great and rapidly rose to be one of the greatest seaports of the ancient world. From 323-30BC it was the capital of Egypt and acquired magnificent buildings (including the famous lighthouse, one of the seven wonders of the ancient world), thriving industries and prosperous banks. Alexandria attracted people from the whole Greek-speaking world as well as native Egyptians. Palestine is Egypt's immediate neighbour to the north and the main land routes passed through it, so it is not surprising that there was a large Jewish population by the dawn of the Christian era, with its own quarter administered by its own Jewish ruler.

It was natural, therefore, for Joseph to take Mary and the infant Jesus to Egypt, where he would easily be able to earn his living until a time when they could safely

The Flight into Egypt
Edward Burne-Jones (1833–98),
Chapel at Castle Howard,
Yorkshire.

This stained-glass panel shows the influence of the pre-Raphaelite movement's attempts to return to the simplicity of early Italian art. It depicts Joseph, Mary and the infant Jesus, against a stylized background of Jerusalem, setting out on their journey to escape from King Herod.

return to their home in Nazareth. In his account of this episode, Matthew takes the opportunity to allude to a common feature of the Messianic prophecies, in which the Messiah reenacts the stay of the ancient Israelites in Egypt, and their journey back to the promised land: 'Out of Egypt have I called my son.'

When he arose, he took the young child and his mother by night, and departed into Egypt, and was there until the death of Herod: that it might be fulfilled which was spoken of the Lord by the prophet, saying, Out of Egypt have I called my son.

Matt 2:14-15, citing Hosea 11:1

THE SLAUGHTER OF
THE INNOCENTS

Then Herod, when he saw that he was mocked of the wise men,
was exceeding wroth, and sent forth, and slew all the children
that were in Bethlehem, and in all the coasts thereof, from two
years old and under, according to the time which he had
diligently inquired of the wise men.

Matt 2:16

According to Matthew, all the male children of Bethlehem below the
age of two were killed by order of King Herod the Great because of
reports that a king had been born there. As this is the only source for
this massacre, some have tried to discount it on the grounds that such an event would be
widely reported, and the people would not permit a ruler to commit such an atrocity.

The Jewish historian and soldier Josephus is the only other local source for this
period, and he records so many of Herod's atrocities – and achievements – that the
slaughter of a few children in a small town becomes insignificant compared with them.
Herod was appointed King of the Jews by the Roman senate in 40BC to wrest control of
Palestine from the Parthians who had invaded with the support of the Egyptian Queen
Cleopatra. He was successful and ruled for 33 years under the Roman governor of the
province of Syria. Herod filled his kingdom with impressive building works, ranging
from the great port he built at Caesarea on the Mediterranean, to his magnificent
renewal of the Hebrew Temple in Jerusalem.

Extremely suspicious of any threat to his power, Herod also constructed massive

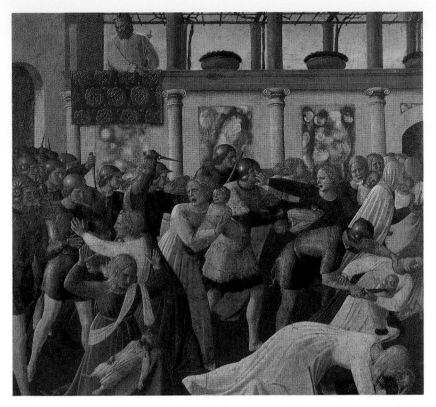

The Massacre of the Innocents
Fra Angelico (c1400–1455),
Museo di San Marco dell'Angelico,
Florence.

Commissioned by Piero d'Medici in 1450 as one of 35 scenes from the life
of Christ on a silver chest for the Santissima Annunciata church in
Florence, this depicts the slaughter of the children of Bethlehem ordered
by Herod the Great following the birth of Jesus.

fortresses at strategic positions throughout the kingdom, including Masada overlooking
the Dead Sea, for his own protection against the people he ruled. He ruthlessly
suppressed any hint of opposition and even had his wives and most of his own children
executed. Herod died as he lived, for the news that he was dying prompted two rabbis to
destroy a golden eagle Herod had erected over the Great Gate of the Temple in defiance
of Hebrew law. Herod summoned enough strength to have the rabbis burned alive and
their helpers executed. He himself died shortly afterwards.

Matthew quotes cryptically from the prophet Jeremiah, alluding to Rachel weeping
for her dead children, to illustrate the slaughter of the innocents, but his Jewish
Christian readers would have no difficulty in recognizing the reference. Rachel died
somewhere near Bethlehem, where her name was especially revered (Ruth 4:11), and the
Jeremiah passage moves straight on into a promise that her children would return. Not
only, therefore, does the passage carry allusions to Bethlehem, it also implies that the
slaughtered children would share in the resurrection of the infant in whose stead they
had been killed.

*A Winter Scene with Massacre of the
Innocents*
Pieter Brueghel the Younger
(c1564–1638), Sotheby's, London
(overleaf).

In the most pointed of comments
on contemporary politics,
Brueghel depicts Herod's
slaughter of the children of
Bethlehem as an atrocity
committed by Spanish soldiers in
a Flemish village.

THE BOY JESUS IN
THE TEMPLE

And it came to pass, that after three days they found him in the
temple, sitting in the midst of the doctors, both hearing them,
and asking them questions. And all that heard him were
astonished at his understanding and answers.

Luke 2:46-47

When King Herod's reign ended the Romans honoured Herod's will
by dividing his kingdom between the three sons who had managed
to survive him and to retain his murderously unpredictable favour.
The holy family returned to Nazareth in Galilee, now part of the area ruled by Herod
Antipas, where Luke records that Jesus grew strong in spirit, filled with wisdom and the
grace of God. When Jesus was twelve, he accompanied his parents on a pilgrimage to
the Temple in Jerusalem, where they lost him.

The Temple itself was a comparatively small building consisting of two main rooms
and a vestibule. Worshippers had access to a series of courtyards surrounding the
Temple, the innermost only for priests, then successive courtyards for men, women, and
Gentiles. The whole complex stood on a great stone platform at the northern end of old
Jerusalem. Apart from the regular daily round of sacrifices in the Temple building and
its forecourt, the outer courtyards were places where anyone could teach or talk.

Hebrew law required all Jews to make the pilgrimage to Jerusalem three times a year
for the greater festivals, but those living at a distance had only to go for Passover, and
many would be unable to manage even that. Joseph and Mary made the annual

Christus in the Temple
Bernard van Orley (c1488–1541),
Burghley House, Stamford,
England.

Court painter to Margaret of Austria, Regent of the Netherlands, Orley
depicts the only incident recorded about Jesus between his infancy and his
public ministry. Aged twelve, Jesus is in discussion with scholars in the
Temple in Jerusalem and amazing them with his understanding.

pilgrimage, probably with many others from Nazareth, and on this occasion at least they
took Jesus with them. On their way home they found he was missing. When they
returned to Jerusalem, full of anxiety, they found he was still in the Temple complex,
engaged in discussion with the Temple scholars.

No more need be read into this incident than a highly intelligent boy engaged in
fascinated discussion with good teachers, but the incident provides the first recorded
words of Jesus: 'Wist ye not that I must be about my Father's business?'

This one incident is the only information in the gospels about 'the silent years',
which stretch from the infancy of Jesus to the beginning of his public ministry at about
the age of 33.

THE PREACHING OF
JOHN THE BAPTIST

John had his raiments of camel's hair, and a leathern girdle about his loins; and his meat was locusts and wild honey. Then went out to him Jerusalem and all Judaea, and all the region about Jordan, and were baptized of him in Jordan, confessing their sins.

Matt 3:4-6

Round about AD27 a man in his early thirties was attracting large crowds to the arid district east of Jerusalem where the River Jordan enters the Dead Sea. John the Baptist's personal austerity matched the message he preached and emphasized its credibility. The people who came to listen to him knew that for many years John had rejected ordinary comforts to survive on the sparse provisions of the desolate area he had made his home.

By then the Emperor Tiberius had ruled for 15 years, and Palestine had been part of a Roman province for nearly 100 years. To ordinary Jews this meant layers of taxation by Roman governors, by their own Jewish kings appointed by Rome, and by the religious leaders in Jerusalem. Tax collecting was farmed out to contractors who notoriously took what they could extort, backed by troops. Abuses and poverty abounded for preachers like John the Baptist to denounce.

John's audience recognized that he belonged to the ancient Hebrew prophetic tradition of such men as Elijah, Amos, Isaiah and Jeremiah. He feared no one and denounced corruption and injustice wherever it was to be found: in rulers and people, priests and laity, lawless soldiers and their victims alike. His outspokenness finally cost him his life at the hands of King Herod Antipas (*see* Mark 6:17-29).

St. John the Baptist in the Wilderness
Sir John Soane's Museum.

This enchanting page from an
illuminated manuscript relates to
the Feast of John the Bapist. It
depicts John with wild animals in
the wilderness near the River
Jordan, where he urges people to
prepare for the coming of the
Messiah. He is pointing to a lamb
with a halo and a cross, one of the
symbols for Jesus.

The shores of the Dead Sea supported a number of devout religious communities,
such as the Essenes of the 'Dead Sea Scrolls' at Qumran, and John may well have been
influenced by them. Baptism was already practised in Judaism for adult converts, and
ritual bathing was a prominent feature of the Qumran community. But when John
baptized people he said that it symbolized repentance and the remission of sins (Mark
1:4). Moreover, he claimed that he was only preparing the way for someone mightier
than himself who would baptize with the Holy Ghost and fire. John meant his cousin,
Jesus.

THE BAPTISM OF JESUS

Then cometh Jesus from Galilee to Jordan unto John, to be baptized of him. But John forbad him, saying, I have need to be baptized of thee, and comest thou to me? And Jesus answering said unto him, Suffer it to be so now, for thus it becometh us to fulfil all righteousness.

Matt 3:13-15

The baptism of Jesus by his cousin, John the Baptist, marked the start of his public ministry. It was a strange way to begin it, for John taught that his baptism was for people who knew that they were sinners in need of forgiveness by God. When Jesus presented himself for baptism, John protested to Jesus that he had no need of baptism; indeed, it was Jesus who should be baptizing John.

By this protest, John the Baptist indicated that Jesus was the Messiah, the long awaited saviour sent by God to free the world from its sins. John urged people to repent because the kingdom of heaven was near; Jesus was the sign that it had arrived. John continued his ministry of preparing people for the impact of Jesus, but he would soon be saying that it was time for him to fade from the scene and leave the work to Jesus.

John the Baptist referred to Jesus as the Lamb of God who had come to take away the sins of the world. The allusion is to the annual Passover ritual, and to the daily round of sacrifices held in the Temple in Jerusalem, both of which helped the worshippers to

The Baptism of Christ
Piero della Francesca
(*c*1420–1492), National Gallery,
London.

In this early work, Piero depicts John the Baptist baptising Jesus against
an Umbrian landscape, watched by angels. The dove above Jesus's head
represents the Holy Spirit which Jesus saw descending upon him after he
had been baptized.

bridge the chasm between God and the world. Jewish law required that the sacrificial lambs should be without blemish.

Jesus insisted on being baptized by John as if he was scarred by sin and in need of forgiveness. By so doing he associated himself as closely as possible with the sinful world he had come to save, and demonstrated that he really had 'made himself of no reputation' as the first Christians expressed it (Phil 2:7). The crucifixion, when it came, would only be the final phase of the abasement Jesus accepted publicly at his baptism.

Despite his misgivings about doing it, John the Baptist baptized Jesus. The phenomena experienced by Jesus during his baptism marked the extraordinary character of the event.

The opening of the heavens echoed a prayer in Isaiah that God would tear the heavens apart and come down to rescue his people again, just as he had done when he rescued them from their slavery in Egypt. The descent of the Holy Spirit in the form of a dove contained allusions to the Spirit of God which came to the Israelites at the great covenant and accompanied them on their journey to the promised land. And the dove itself was an ancient biblical symbol for the Hebrew people.

The voice from heaven proclaimed Jesus as God's son in terms which echoed the 'servant' poems of Isaiah and elements of the coronation rite of the Hebrew kings. The 'servant' in Isaiah was to be God's agent for bringing true justice to the world, and he would suffer death in the process. The coronation rite spoke of God giving the king the nations as his birthright, and the whole world as his possession. The baptism of Jesus became the occasion when he was assured that this was the beginning of the final, decisive phase in God's plan to reconcile the world to himself again.

How Jesus went about that task would be quite different from anything his followers expected. The Messianic prophecies spoke of an invincible hero who would bring God's people peace and political freedom, and wreak vengeance on their enemies. Even John the Baptist began to have doubts as Jesus failed to fulfil popular expectations. John had been imprisoned by Herod Antipas for criticizing him and from his prison John sent messengers to ask Jesus if he really was the Messiah. Jesus sent them back to tell John about the miracles of healing and the message of hope Jesus was giving to the poor. Throughout his ministry Jesus was faced with the problem of convincing his followers that his methods were the right way for the Messiah to bring in the Messianic age, but few of them were really convinced until after his death and resurrection.

The Baptism of Christ
The Baptistry of Arians, Ravenna.
(right).

The octagonal baptistry next to the cathedral in Ravenna, which may have been adapted from Roman baths, contains magnificent 5th-century mosaics. This one shows a naked Jesus rising from the water after baptism, with the Holy Spirit descending on him and God the Father proclaiming him his son.

And Jesus, when he was baptized, went up straightway out of
the water: and, lo, the heavens were opened unto him, and he
saw the Spirit of God descending like a dove, and lighting upon
him: And lo a voice from heaven, saying, This is my beloved
Son, in whom I am well pleased.

Matt 3:16-17

THE TEMPTATION OF JESUS

And he was there in the wilderness forty days, tempted of Satan; and was with the wild beasts; and the angels ministered unto him.

Mark 1:13

Right at the beginning of his public ministry the gospels report that Jesus had his most prolonged encounter with evil, and successfully resisted it. Mark says that the adversary was named Satan, Matthew and Luke that it was the Devil.

Both Judaism and Christianity have resisted the idea that the forces of evil are independent and equal in power to God. No monotheistic religion could accept such a belief, and Luke's account of the temptation makes it clear that the Devil's powers were derived from God even if they were then used for evil purposes.

In the Book of Job, Satan is a servant of God whose function is to demonstrate how strong God's servants can be in the face of adversity. Like a modern trial lawyer or a test pilot, Satan tested Job with repeated misfortune so that God was able to prove that Job's faithfulness was not based on any material benefits. A similar idea lay behind the temptations of Jesus. They demonstrated that he could not be diverted from his Messianic mission nor from the means that he had chosen to achieve it.

The three temptations all proposed ways in which Jesus might use the power at his disposal for his own selfish ends or for merely mundane purposes. In the first the Devil suggested that Jesus should perform miracles to meet normal material needs, such as food. Jesus replied that the revealed word of God was more important, and thereby

The Temptation of Christ
The Master of St Severin, Victoria
and Albert Museum, London.

The early-16th-century German
stained-glass panel of the Cologne
school depicts the Devil's three
temptations Jesus resisted: to turn
stones to bread; to prove his
divinity by jumping from the
Temple without harm; and to gain
possession of all the kingdoms of
the world by worshipping the
Devil.

implied that any miracles he might perform must serve the truth he had come to reveal. In the second temptation Jesus was asked to prove that he was the son of God by throwing himself from the height of the Temple in Jerusalem to show that he could not come to harm; such a sign would surely compel belief in everyone who saw it. Jesus replied that people must not try to force God to protect them against deliberately rash acts. Finally, the Devil offered Jesus power over the whole world if he would worship him. Jesus replied that God alone is to be worshipped, and ordered Satan away.

Everything that happened to Jesus during the temptations was also a symbol of Jesus's beliefs about his mission. All the replies he gave consisted of quotations from ancient Hebrew religious law, so demonstrating that whatever he did would be faithful to the principles already revealed by God. His task was to fulfil the law and God's promises enshrined in it, not to break it.

The temptations, and the replies given by Jesus, also defined the nature of his mission and the way he intended to achieve it. He would not be diverted into using his powers to satisfy material needs, for that would be to worship a false god. The human need was far deeper. He would not use miracles to force people into believing in him, but only in the face of their immediate needs and in association with their faith in him. Above all, he would not call on any suspect means or powers to gain his ends; everything he achieved would be by unswerving loyalty to God.

One of the most vivid metaphors for temptation, concealed in the derivation of one the Greek words for temptation used in the gospels, is that of the gold refiner. The metal is heated to melting point and beyond in a furnace, so that any impurites float to the surface as dross where they can be skimmed off. The pure gold is undamaged by the melting, and its worth is proved. So too with the temptations of Jesus. They proved that whatever he did was a pure expression of the love and will of God.

JESUS BEGINS HIS MINISTRY

Now after that John was put in prison, Jesus came into Galilee, preaching the gospel of the kingdom of God, and saying, The time is fulfilled, and the kingdom of God is at hand: repent ye, and believe the gospel.

Mark 1:14-15

Shortly after baptizing Jesus, John the Baptist was arrested by King Herod Antipas and imprisoned in the fortress of Machaerus. Jesus accepted it as a sign that he should begin his public ministry. He was aged about 33 and he moved from his small home town of Nazareth to the nearby town of Capernaum on the shores of the Sea of Galilee. By local standards, Capernaum was an important centre with a customs post and a Roman military garrison commanded by a centurion. It was also a base and market for local fishermen, some of whom became disciples of Jesus.

Galilee was an appropriate place for Jesus to begin preaching a message of universal salvation, for two of the busiest of all international routes converged just north of the Sea of Galilee and passed along its western shore on their way to Egypt. The Jews of Jerusalem contemptuously referred to it as 'Galilee of the Gentiles' because of the mixture of peoples left behind by armies and travellers down the centuries.

The message Jesus preached was direct and to the point: the long years of waiting were over and the kingdom of God had arrived. It was a proclamation of 'good news' - the literal meaning of the English word 'gospel', and anyone could benefit from it by repenting and believing. The brief summary of his first teaching does not say what Jesus expected his listeners to believe, but he soon made this clear when he returned to Nazareth to preach in the synagogue where he was so well known.

For his text, Jesus chose a passage from Isaiah which lists the benefits the Messiah will bring: liberty for prisoners, sight for the blind, and hope for all who are oppressed or deprived. He then implied that he himself was the fulfilment of this prophecy. His old neighbours were impressed by his eloquence but the subsequent discussion developed into a fierce argument until they dismissed his claims as blasphemous arrogance. Jesus was lucky to escape with his life as his townsfolk tried to throw him from a nearby cliff.

THE CALL OF THE DISCIPLES

And Jesus said unto Simon, Fear not; from henceforth thou
shalt catch men. And when they had brought their ships to land,
thay forsook all, and followed him.

Luke 5:10-11

I t was remarkable that the people Jesus chose to be most closely associated with
him were none of them priests or qualified experts in the Hebrew religion. As
ordinary Jews, they would have been taught the Jewish scriptures and the
religious significance of their history, and they inherited a rich religious tradition
enshrined in the yearly round of festivals. But none of them were specially trained in the
way we now expect of religious leaders.

Some of them had been disciples of John the Baptist, for John pointed Jesus out to
two of them as the Lamb of God and they followed him to his home. Indeed, in one
version it was Andrew who first took Peter to Jesus after telling him that they had found
the Messiah. The next day Jesus recruited Philip and Nathanael.

As soon as his reputation began to grow, Jesus asked his disciples to join him and
began to extend his teaching campaign. Simon Peter and his brother Andrew, and the
brothers James and John, sons of Zebedee, were called from casting their nets on the
shore of the Sea of Galilee. Matthew was called from the table where he was busy
collecting taxes. More followed, and Luke reports that at one point Jesus appointed at
least 70 disciples.

After about a year Jesus chose twelve from this larger group to be more closely
associated with him. Their function was to help him with his work and to learn to think
as Jesus thought. Shortly after calling them, Jesus boarded the boat of Andrew and Peter
to address a large crowd of people on the beach. Afterwards the two disciples set to
fishing under the guidance of Jesus, and hauled so large a catch that the nets began to
break and they had to call for another boat to help. Even so, both boats began to sink
under the weight of fish and Peter recognized it as a miracle. Jesus told them not to be
afraid; from now onwards they would be fishing for people.

Jesus, walking by the Sea of Galilee, saw two brethren, Simon called Peter, and Andrew his brother, casting a net into the sea: for they were fishers. And he saith unto them, Follow me, and I will make you fishers of men. And they straightway left their nets and followed him.

Matt 4:18-20

The Miraculous Draught of Fishes
Raphael Sanzio (1483–1520)
Victoria and Albert Museum,
London.

Immediately after addressing a
crowd from Peter's boat, Jesus
told him to go further out and
fish. The miraculously large catch
terrified Peter, but Jesus
reassured him and told him and
his partners that from then
onwards they would be fishers of
men.

51

THE MIRACLE AT CANA

Jesus saith unto them, Fill the waterpots with water, and they filled them up to the brim. And he saith unto them, Draw out now, and bear unto the governor of the feast. And they bare it.

When the ruler of the feast had tasted the water that was made wine, and knew not whence it was: (but the servants which drew the water knew;) the governor of the feast called the bridegroom, and saith unto him, Every man at the beginning doth set forth good wine; and when men have well drunk, then that which is worse: but thou hast kept the good wine until now.

John 2: 7-10

Jesus miraculously turned water into wine for no more reason than to save a wedding from turning into an embarrassment. It was probably a family occasion, for Jesus and his mother Mary were present – Joseph fades out of the accounts after the childhood of Jesus – and Mary may well have been helping to organize it. Towards the end of the festivities they ran out of wine and Mary turned to Jesus, perhaps to ask him and his disciples to go quickly and look for more wine in the town. Jesus made it clear to Mary (in words more courteous than appears from the English, 'Woman, what have I to do with thee?') that he was no longer under her authority. He was already obeying a higher authority, even if the hour had not yet come for his final act of obedience on Calvary. So whatever he now did to save the wedding festivities would reveal a deeper pattern than that of a resourceful son helping his mother in a minor crisis.

The Marriage Feast at Cana
Bartolomé-Esteban Murillo
(1617–1682), Barber Institute,
Birmingham.

In sharp contrast to the direct
simplicity of Giotto, the Spanish
painter Murillo sets the scene in
the height of Spanish prosperity
during the period following the
expulsion of Islam and the
European discovery of the
Americas in 1492.

The Marriage Feast at Cana
Giotto di Bondone (c1267–1337),
Scrovegni Chapel, Padua.

In this fresco, part of the great
series commissioned in 1306,
Giotto depicts the first miracle
recorded in John's Gospel. Jesus
turns water into wine to save a
wedding feast to which he, his
mother and the disciples had been
invited.

Jesus told the servants to fill the great stone jars where water was stored for the ritual
purifications required by Hebrew law, and then to draw the water out again and take it
into the feast. They did so, and found they were bearing wine. The six jars between them
would have held more than 100 gallons.

John's Gospel says that the miracles of Jesus were signs which revealed something
about his 'glory', one of the main words in the Bible for the presence and power of God.
It selects this miracle as the first of the seven signs it presents. It had an immediate
effect on the disciples Jesus had gathered round him. They already appreciated that he
was a gifted teacher; now they began to believe that he was at least a prophet who could
do the kind of miracles recorded of Moses. It was a further step towards their full
appreciation of who Jesus really was.

The Marriage Feast at Cana
Paolo Veronese (c1528–1588),
Louvre, Paris.

Veronese's most famous picture
was commissioned in 1562 for the
refectory of S. Georgio Maggiore
in Venice. Among the 120 figures
depicted with Jesus at the feast are
portraits of Queen Mary of
England, Francis I, Charles V,
Titian and the artist himself.

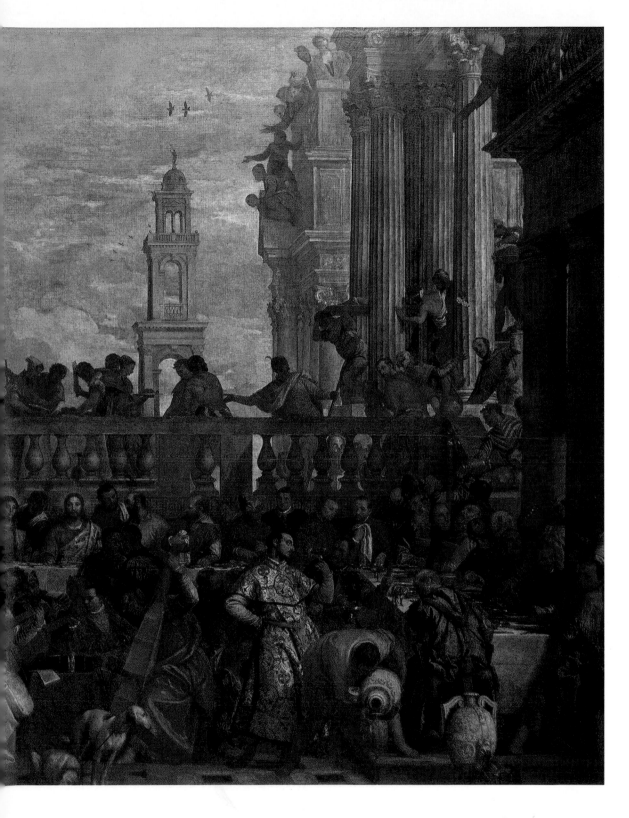

THE FIRST VISIT TO JERUSALEM

Take these things hence; make not my Father's house an house
of merchandise.

John 2:16

John's Gospel records that the first visit of the adult Jesus to Jerusalem was for
a celebration of the Passover, accompanied by his disciples. There he visited
the great Temple, the only place in the world where the Hebrew religious
law permitted animal sacrifices to be offered, and found that the outer courts were
crowded with traders serving the needs of pilgrims.

Worshippers needed animals for the sacrifices commanded by the law, mainly sheep
and oxen, but people too poor to be able to provide such expensive offerings were
allowed to use pigeons. Joseph and Mary sacrificed two pigeons after the birth of Jesus.
Incense and grain were also needed for some sacrifices. The religious taxes collected in
the Temple had to be paid in coins minted in Tyre, which had a higher silver content
than the Roman coins, and money-changers operated within the Temple precincts to
serve this special need.

Whether the various traders made exorbitant profits is not stated, but Jesus took
objection to their presence because they were turning 'my Father's house' into a market.
He drove them out with a whip, scattered the money and overturned the stalls.

The Temple authorities seemed remarkably restrained in their reactions, for they only
asked Jesus to produce some 'sign' of his authority. 'Destroy this temple,' replied Jesus,
'and in three days I will raise it up!' As the reconstruction work had already taken 46
years the reply must have appeared impertinent, but Jesus had attracted a large
following and the authorities allowed him to leave.

After his resurrection – three days after his death – his disciples remembered the
answer he had given and realized that he was referring to his own body. Jesus himself
was the Temple, the place of God's presence, the centre of worship and the sacrifice
itself. But no one could have been expected to understand that or to accept it as he drove
out the Temple traders.

The other three gospels record a similar incident when Jesus drove traders out of the
Temple during the last week of his life, which many scholars think is the same one.

JESUS AND
NICODEMUS

A man of the Pharisees, named Nicodemus, came to Jesus by
night, and said unto him, Rabbi, we know that thou art a
teacher come from God: for no man can do these miracles that
thou doest, except God be with him. Jesus answered, Verily,
verily, I say unto thee, Except a man be born again, he cannot
see the kingdom of God.

John 3:1-3

Not everyone who wanted to approach Jesus could do so openly, for
Jesus soon aroused the suspicion and opposition of the main Jewish
religious parties. Nicodemus was not only a prominent Pharisee – a
powerfully influencial group which insisted on rigorous interpretation of the law – he
was also a member of the Sanhedrin, the supreme court for Judaism.

Although occupied by the Romans, the Jews were allowed to run much of the
government of Jerusalem and Judaea, and to influence the lives of Jews throughout the
Roman world. They did this through the Great Council, the Sanhedrin. The high priest
presided over it, and its membership came from tribal leaders, legal experts, and the two
main religious parties, the Pharisees and Sadduccees. As a member of the Sanhedrin,
Nicodemus could not risk being seen with Jesus, so he went to him under cover of
darkness.

Jesus took him seriously, and answered the question which lay concealed in what
Nicodemus actually said to him. Jesus told him that he must be born again if he really
wanted to accept what Jesus taught. It was a strange expression for anyone to use, and
Nicodemus asked Jesus what he meant; surely not to enter the womb again?

No, said Jesus, it meant that he must be born of water and the spirit to escape from
the 'flesh'; the corruptions and limitations of human nature. Jesus was saying that it was
not enough to be impressed by his teaching, or even by his power to do miracles. There
must also be a spiritual rebirth, sealed by baptism.

Jesus went on to say that there was nothing exclusive about this. He had been sent
not to condemn the world, but to bring the world back to God. All who were genuinly
committed to the truth would share in the light Jesus brought into the world, and they
would be assured that what they did came from God.

THE SAMARITAN
WOMAN AT THE WELL

There cometh a woman of Samaria to draw water: Jesus saith unto her, Give me to drink. Then saith the woman of Samaria unto him, How is it that thou, being a Jew, asketh drink of me, which am a woman of Samaria? for the Jews have no dealings with the Samaritans.

John 4:7-9

The exchange between Jesus and the woman at the well is one of the most entertaining and vivid in the gospels. Jesus was alone, for his disciples had gone to buy provisions, and the woman was alone at a well outside her town; that itself in those times made her unconventional.

Jesus asked her to draw him water and she lightly chided him with being a Jew who asked something of a Samaritan. For at least 500 years Jews had despised their neighbours in Samaria (*see* 'The Good Samaritan'). Jesus told her that if she knew who he was she would have begged water of him and he would have given her living water. The woman continued her banter: Jesus had no bucket; where would he get living water? Was he greater than Jacob, who dug the well?

To take it deeper than banter, Jesus asked her to fetch her husband, and when she said that she had no husband he revealed that he knew all about her life as a prostitute. At this the woman herself turned the exchange to matters of religion. Why did Jews like Jesus insist that everyone should go to Jerusalem to sacrifice, when she and her ancestors had always worshipped on the holy mountain behind her town? The time would soon

58

Christ with the Samaritan Woman
Musée des Augustins, Toulouse.

The 16th-century stone sculpture
is inspired by the meeting
between Jesus and a woman at a
well outside a town in Samaria.
What began as a light-hearted
exchange ended with the woman
acknowledging Jesus as the
Messiah.

come, replied Jesus, when people would worship 'in spirit and in truth' wherever they
were, without need of Jerusalem or holy mountains.

By now the woman was impressed, and expressed her belief and hope in the promised
Messiah who would reveal all things. Jesus said, 'I that speak unto thee am he.'

What had started as a simple request for a drink and a little light-hearted banter,
ended with the town asking Jesus and his disciples to stay. They spent two days there,
and many of the people believed because, as they said, they had now heard him
themselves and knew that he was the Christ, the Saviour of the world.

59

THE MURDER OF
JOHN THE BAPTIST

When Herod's birthday was kept, the daughter of Herodias
danced before them, and pleased Herod. Whereupon he
promised with an oath to give her whatsoever she would ask.

And she, being before instructed by her mother, said, Give
me here John Baptist's head in a charger.

Matt 14:6-8

The gospels do not say just when John the Baptist was murdered, but they record the terrible event because Herod thought Jesus might be John come back from the dead. It is no surprise that so vivid an event has inspired so many artists, musicians and poets.

The Herod in question was Antipas, the sixth son of Herod the Great, who inherited the rule of Galilee and an area east of the River Jordan. He divorced his first wife in order to marry Herodias, the wife of a half- brother, and John the Baptist denounced this marriage as unlawful. Herod clapped John in prison at the great fortress of Machaerus overlooking the Dead Sea, and it was there that John was executed.

The gospels also hint that Herod feared the large following that John had attracted by his preaching. Armed rebellion was always a possibility and many of the risings had religious associations in a country where the people were expecting a military Messiah modelled on King David. All the Herods tried to crush any sign of opposition before it had any chance of succeeding, and Herod Antipas was no different.

Herodias, with the Head of John the Baptist
Elizabeth Sirani (1638–1665),
Burghley House, Stamford,
Lincolnshire.

The young artist has concentrated on Salome's mother Herodias, who married Herod Antipas after being divorced from his brother. Herodias was determined to have her revenge on John the Baptist for his public criticism of her and Herod.

The Head of John the Baptist
Anton Andreievitch Ivanoff
(1815–1848), Tretyakov Gallery,
Moscow.

Herod Antipas, son of the
notorious Herod the Great,
imprisoned John the Baptist for
condemning his illegal marriage.
A rash public promise at a feast
led him reluctantly to having
John beheaded.

The well-known scene was a birthday feast for Herod Antipas at which Herodias's daughter (by Herod's half-brother) danced. The gospels do not name her, but she is usually identified as Salome. Herod was entranced and promised her anything she asked. By previous arrangement with her mother Herodias, she asked for John the Baptist's head to be given her on a serving dish.

To give Herod his due, he was reluctant to give the girl her wish. He had great respect for John, and he may well have been worried about the unrest his execution might provoke, but he had sworn a solemn oath before his entire household. He dared not lose face or appear afraid, even though the girl had used his rash promise to grant her mother's vengeful wish. John's head was given to her, and she gave it to her mother. Herodias had obtained her revenge for John's criticism of her.

The Dance of Salome
Benozzo Gozzoli (*c*1421–1497),
Kress Collection, Washington
D.C.

The Florentine-born painter, strongly influenced by Fra Angelico, has
included three successive parts of the incident in the painting: Salome's
dance and Herod's rash promise to her; John the Baptist being beheaded;
and the girl presenting the head to her mother, Herodias.

And the king was sorry: nevertheless for the oath's sake, and
them which sat with him at meat, he commanded it to be given
her. And he sent, and beheaded John in the prison.
And his head was brought in a charger, and given to the damsel:
and she brought it to her mother.

Matt 14:9-11

THE CURE OF THE
PARALYTIC

And they come unto him, bringing one sick of the palsy, which
was borne of four. And when they could not come nigh unto him
for the press, they uncovered the roof where he was: and when
they had broken it up, they let down the bed wherein the sick of
the palsy lay. When Jesus saw their faith, he said unto the sick
of the palsy, Son, thy sins be forgiven thee.

Mark 2:3-5

When Jesus returned with his disciples to start work in earnest in
Galilee, his reputation grew so rapidly that some people could not
get near him for the crowds. More than once the gospels record
that he took to a boat, or tried to escape to a desert place to be alone.

On this occasion four men carrying a paralysed friend on a stretcher found they could
only reach Jesus by digging a hole in the flat roof of the house where he was staying in
Capernaum, and letting their friend down on ropes. But Jesus saw a need deeper than
the man's paralysis; moved by his faith and the faith of his friends, Jesus told him that
his sins were forgiven.

Whatever effect Jesus's words had on the paralytic and his friends, the scribes present
reacted angrily. These were highly skilled professional writers, whose work ranged from
the kind of government administration now performed by civil servants, to the
production of scrolls of the sacred scriptures. They were held in high esteem, and they
were considered to be expert religious teachers. Perhaps their presence shows that the

Christ healing the Paralytic at
Capernaum
Kariye Camii, Istanbul.

The paralysed man had been brought to Jesus by four friends. When they found they could not get near him for the crowds, they made a hole in the roof and let him down at Jesus's feet. Jesus forgave his sins and then, as the 14th-century mosaic shows, he healed him.

religious authorities were already worried about Jesus. The scribes were offended because the Hebrew religion held that only God could forgive sins, but Jesus had spoken as if he himself had authority to forgive. The act could be interpreted as a blasphemous claim to divinity, and the scribes chose to interpret it as such.

Knowing what the scribes were thinking, Jesus told the paralysed man to get up, pick up his stretcher and walk. The man immediately did so. Jesus performed the visible miracle to authenticate the deeper miracle; he removed the man's paralysis to show that he had removed the man's sins. The incident provoked the first signs of opposition to Jesus by the religious authorities, which would finally culminate in his legal condemnation on a charge of blasphemy.

THE SERMON ON THE MOUNT AND AFTER

And seeing the multitudes, he went up into a mountain. And when he was set, his disciples came unto him: and he opened his mouth, and taught them, saying,

Blessed are the poor in spirit: for theirs is the kingdom of heaven.

Blessed are they that mourn: for they shall be comforted.

Blessed are the meek: for they shall inherit the earth.

Matt 5:1-5

The famous 4th century African bishop, St. Augustine, called the Sermon on the Mount the perfect rule or pattern of Christian life, and subsequent generations of Christians have confirmed his judgement. For three chapters, Matthew's Gospel presents the heart of Jesus's teaching in a collection of pithy sayings, parables and new interpretations of ancient Hebrew law. It also contains the best known of all Christian prayers, the Lord's Prayer: 'Our Father which art in heaven ...'

Whether or not Jesus gave this address on a Galilean hillside exactly as it has come down to us, there can be no doubt that it sums up his teaching in the words he used. It was addressed to the disciples, but it is clear from the ending that a large crowd was also there, so its teaching was not meant exclusively for a spiritual elite, but for anyone who was prepared to listen to Jesus.

The Beatitudes with which it opens – so named because each one begins 'blessed are ...'

Sermon on the Mount
B. Angelico, Museo di S. Marco,
Firenze.

The painting refers to the long
discourse reported in Matthew's
Gospel when Jesus preached on a
hillside near the sea of Galilee.

Think not that I am come to destroy the law, or the prophets: I
am not come to destroy but to fulfil. For verily I say unto you,
Till heaven and earth pass, one jot or one tittle shall in no wise
pass from the law, till all be fulfilled.

Matt 5:17-18

— sum up the basic theme of the whole address: the quality of life expected of those who
wish to be citizens of the kingdom of God. They accept their own weakness and they
know they will be strengthened in times of special need. They are meek; they hunger
and thirst for righteousness; they are merciful and peacemakers. They are not surprised if
their loyalty to God's truth brings them persecution, for the prophets had the same
experience, and they can be confident that their reward awaits them in heaven.

Such people were the salt of the earth, said Jesus, and the light of the world; they
were like a city set on a hilltop where all can see it. The listeners would think
immediately of the fortified hill towns of Palestine, where people working the
surrounding fields could flee from danger. But the salt must be kept uncontaminated,
and the light must be visible, and the city must be strong. Jesus made it clear that his
followers must live lives which attracted others to him.

In the most surprising section of the Sermon on the Mount Jesus related his own

The Sermon on the Mount
Cosimo Rosselli (1439–1507),
Sistine Chapel, The Vatican.

One of four frescoes the Florentine
Rosselli painted on the walls of
the Sistine Chapel in 1481 and
1482, this depicts Jesus
addressing a crowd in a very
Italianate landscape.

teaching to the traditional Hebrew law which the Old Testament says was dictated in all its detail by God to Moses. Jesus asserted emphatically that his mission and teaching was in full support of the law, not a defiance of it and still less a threat to it. Even so, the effects were dramatic, and they led to the Christian rejection of the Hebrew code of law as the essential way to being right with God.

Jesus tackled the law by going behind the letter of it to the principles it enshrined. Observing the principles of the law was far removed from the narrow legalism of the scribes and Pharisees who concentrated on keeping the letter of it. Jesus roundly condemned their form of 'righteousness' and said it actually prevented people from entering the kingdom of heaven.

In the Sermon on the Mount Jesus took a number of examples from Hebrew law to show what he meant by keeping the law. The first was the commandment 'Thou shalt not kill'. The evil this condemned was anger, so any form of anger was a breach of the law, not just anger which led to killing. Jesus said that his followers should not even worship until they were reconciled with those who had anything against them.

So too with the laws dealing with adultery, divorce, taking oaths and retribution for personal injury. In each instance there was a principle of perfection which the legal formula could not fully express, and it was all too easy to keep the letter of the law and break the principle it was meant to defend. Lust of any kind was evil, not mere adultery; marriages were permanent relationships and not to be abandoned; there was no need for oaths if every word spoken was true; people should accept injury without seeking retribution.

All that the law sought to uphold could be expressed in terms of love - for enemies as well as friends. 'Be ye therefore perfect, even as your Father which is in heaven is perfect.'

The Lord's Prayer is more famous than anything else Jesus said, and it comes in the section of the Sermon on the Mount where he gave practical directions about the kind of conduct expected of members of the kingdom of heaven. They should practise their good works so secretly that even their left hands did not know what their right hands were doing. They should practise fasting, but be careful to show no external signs of it. They should trust in providence, deal with today's problems and not worry what tomorrow might bring.

The gospels give many examples of Jesus himself praying and exhorting others to pray, but the Lord's Prayer is the only instance where Jesus gave his followers a general formula for prayer. It calls on those who pray to begin by acknowledging the universal authority and holiness of God, and then to ask for him to meet their immediate needs – 'our daily bread'.

The petition for forgiveness in the prayer is unconditional, for it asks that God will forgive worshippers to the extent that they forgive others. In this the prayer is only expressing the practical consequences of the sermon's more general injunction to forgive enemies as well as friends. Jesus emphasized this point immediately after giving his listeners the prayer; if they did not forgive others their sins, he said, their heavenly Father would not forgive them their sins.

'Lead us not into temptation' is the part of the prayer most open to misunderstanding, for the word for 'temptation' refers to legal trials and the kind of tests used to establish the truth. Here the prayer echoes Jesus's own experience when he was led into the desert for the temptations or tests which proved that he was incorruptible. The section in praise of God at the end of the prayer matches the opening of it.

The Lord's Prayer sums up Jesus's teaching about membership of the kingdom of heaven, but it is worth noticing that the gospels never report that Jesus prayed for forgiveness for himself.

At the end of the Sermon on the Mount Matthew's Gospel describes the effect Jesus had on the people who had come to hear him teach. The crowd on the hillside contrasted Jesus with the scribes, and they decided that he spoke with authority, unlike their official religious leaders and teachers. Clearly, they had found his message attractive and full of hope, yet he had not presented them with an easy way of life.

In the final passages Jesus again emphasized that God would judge people by the same standards they themselves showed when they judged others. He attacked hypocrisy

> But when you pray, use not vain repetitions, as the heathen do: for they think that they shall be heard for their much speaking. Be not ye therefore like unto them: for your Father knoweth what things ye have need of, before ye ask him.
>
> After this manner therefore pray ye: Our Father which art in heaven, Hallowed be thy name ...
>
> Matt 6:7-9

with a vivid little parable – do not look for specks in others' eyes when there is a beam of wood in your own eye. And just as the meat of the Temple sacrifices must not be given to dogs, so too his way of life was not for people likely to abuse it.

Jesus had given his listeners a hard message, but he also promised that they would receive all the help they asked for from God: just as parents provided their children with wholesome food, so God gave good things to those who asked him. Jesus continued with a warning that there were teachers who could not be trusted, but he told his audience that they themselves could judge whether or not teachers were authentic: 'by their fruits ye shall know them'. If he had wished, Jesus could have pointed to himself, for the life he led helped to authenticate his teaching.

The sermon ends with Jesus giving his audience another parable: anyone who listened to him and practised what he said was like someone who built a house on foundations of rock. That house would stand in a storm. Whoever listened to Jesus and did not put his teaching into practice was building on sand and the house would fall. In other words, the effectiveness of the teaching depended on whether or not the listener acted on it.

The crowd who heard the Sermon on the Mount were impressed by the sheer authority with which Jesus taught. On the way back to Capernaum Jesus showed his authority in a different way when he was met by two men in need of his power to heal. The first was a leper who simply said that Jesus could heal him if he wished to. Jesus did so. The second was a Roman officer whose servant was ill.

The Roman centurion was no Jew, but he had paid for a Jewish synagogue to be built near his headquarters in Capernaum. When his servant fell ill, he turned to Jesus, a local Jew with a reputation for healing, and confronted him as he entered the town. We are tempted to view it romantically: the Roman in polished leather, plumed helmet and purple cloak; the local Jewish worthies in flowing robes, anxious that their benefactor should be helped; and Jesus gravely listening.

The scene is surprising enough, for the central figure was the local commander of a foreign army of occupation. The Jews themselves had called in the Romans to stop a civil war between Jewish factions, but that need had long since been forgotten. Now the extremists hated the foreign troops and seized every chance to murder them.

The Roman officer had power of command, but his power was not his own. It came from the supreme power of the Roman emperor, delegated to the centurion. The emperor's power was channelled into Galilee through this Roman soldier. That was the kind of authority the centurion recognized in Jesus; absolute power delegated to him by God. He told Jesus that he did not expect him to come to his Gentile house; if Jesus gave the order, the servant would be healed. Whatever evil was harming him, it would be helpless before the supreme power delegated to Jesus.

Surprised by the soldier's insight, Jesus used words which shocked the listening Jews: 'I have not found so great faith, no, not in Israel.'

And it came to pass, when Jesus had ended these sayings, the people were astonished at his doctrine, for he taught them as one having authority, and not as the scribes.

Matt 7:28-29

Lord, my servant lieth at home sick of the palsy, grievously tormented. And Jesus saith unto him, I will come and heal him. The centurion answered and said, Lord, I am not worthy that thou shouldest come under my roof: but speak the word only, and my servant shall be healed.

Matt 8:6-8

A WOMAN ANOINTS JESUS

And, behold, a woman in the city, which was a sinner, when she knew that Jesus sat at meat in the Pharisee's house, brought an alabaster box of ointment, and stood at his feet behind him weeping, and began to wash his feet with tears, and did wipe them with the hairs of her head, and kissed his feet, and anointed them with the ointment.

Luke 7:37-38

Jesus had been invited to a meal by a prominent Galilean Pharisee named Simon, and as he reclined at the table a woman began to weep over his feet and dry them with her hair. She then took an expensive jar of scented oil and poured it over his feet. To those present, the incident might well have seemed no more than a woman's infatuation with Jesus. Despite popular tradition she is unnamed, and there is no good reason to connect her with Mary Magdalene.

Simon the Pharisee was scandalized, for the woman was a notorious prostitute. If Jesus did not already know of her, his famed prophetic insight must tell him what kind of woman she was; why did Jesus allow her to behave in such an outrageous manner? Possibly the precious cosmetic she poured over his feet was associated with her profession. It was a public embarrassment, and Simon showed his indignation.

Jesus answered Simon's criticisms by putting a parable to him: a debtor owed ten times more than another debtor, and neither could pay. The creditor cancelled both debts. Which of the two debtors would be the more grateful? Simon gave the obvious answer, as was expected in the parable method of discussion, and Jesus agreed.

Mary Magdalene Anointing the Feet of Christ in Simon's House Church at Llanwenllwyfro in Anglesey.

The 16th-century Flemish painted glass panel depicts the incident in which a well-known prostitute poured expensive perfume over Jesus's feet as an expression of her penitence, and was forgiven. The gospels do not say that she was Mary Magdalene.

Now Jesus applied the parable to Simon and the woman. As Simon had implied, everyone knew that she had much to be forgiven. By her extravagant actions towards Jesus she showed that she believed that he had forgiven her. Simon, on the other hand, had done no more than ask Jesus to a meal and had not even honoured him with the conventional washing of feet.

There is no reason to doubt Simon's motives: he might have invited Jesus because he also felt the need for forgiveness, but he found it hard to recognize the woman's penitence and that her extravagant act was gratitude for forgiveness.

Jesus turned to the woman and left no one present in any doubt about his own reactions. He told her that her faith in him had saved her, and she could go in peace.

73

THE PARABLE OF
THE SOWER

Behold, there went out a sower to sow: and it came to pass, as he
sowed, some fell by the way side, and the fowls of the air came
and devoured it up. And some fell on stony ground ... and
because it had no root, it withered away.

Mark 4:3-6

Along with the Good Samaritan and the Prodigal Son, the Sower is one
of the best known of all the parables Jesus told. The parable itself is
simply a scene which would have been familiar to any of the people
listening to Jesus, and to anyone familiar with arable farming until industrialization
changed farming practices.

A sower walked through his ploughed field systematically casting the seed by hand
from a bag at his waist. However selective he might be, there were limits to his control
over the fall of seed, and the yield depended on the various kinds of ground. Seed on a
hard path would be eaten by birds; seed among stones would only develop shallow roots
and be easily scorched. Seeds among thorns would be choked. Only the seed which fell
on good ground would yield a good harvest.

Parables only work as a teaching method because they relate to familiar situations
and ask questions with obvious conclusions; then the conclusions can be applied to the
listeners' own lives. But when the disciples were alone with Jesus they asked him what
this parable really meant.

The reply given to them by Jesus indicated the problem: what if the listeners refused
to give the obvious answer because they did not want to accept the consequences for
their own lives? Then, said Jesus, they would have cut themselves off from their only
source of hope. They would never understand and never be healed.

It was a daunting conclusion, hammered home by Jesus in words quoted from the
prophet Isaiah. Jesus had to tell the disciples that he could not help people against their
will. He could only reach those who were willing to face the truth about themselves. As
they would discover, people might even be turned against him by the truths with which
he faced them. As Isaiah had discovered when his warnings were ignored, being called
by God was not a guarantee of success.

THE BEELZEBUB
CHARGE

The scribes which came down from Jerusalem said, He hath
Beelzebub, and by the prince of the devils casteth he out devils.
And he called them unto him, and said unto them in parables,
How can Satan cast out Satan?

Mark 3:22

Very soon during his activities in his home area, Jesus had antagonized
the local religious leaders of Galilee to the point where they felt that
they had to be rid of him. His enemies began to watch him closely for
open breaches of the religious law, but Jesus always managed to appeal to the common
sense of the ordinary people.

Jesus did behave unconventionally, so the questions and arguments put to him by
religious officials were sometimes well justified. It was reasonable for Pharisees to ask
him why he seemed to prefer the company of social outcasts, or to ask him why he was
so careless about keeping the sabbath regulations. But some did see him as a serious
threat to Hebrew religious tradition.

Because of his popularity, it was essential for them to find an argument which would
convince people that Jesus was really evil. It was not an easy task. Most illnesses were
attributed to possession by devils, and Jesus showed such powers to exorcise devils that
the sick flocked to him from far and near. His healing powers reinforced the authority of
his teaching and convinced people that he had been sent by God.

It was scribes from Jerusalem who finally suggested a solution. These professionally
trained experts in the sacred writings suggested that Jesus was a servant of the ultimate
evil, variously referred to as the Devil and named Satan or Beelzebub. It was a clever
explanation, for it could be made to fit any situation: if Jesus overcame devils it was
because he had more evil power than any of them; if he taught convincingly it only
showed how cleverly Satan can deceive.

Jesus said that these arguments only proved that the powers of evil were divided
against themselves and no longer able to do harm. But more seriously, the charge against
him was unforgivable, said Jesus, for it made the Holy Spirit the ultimate evil and used
any sign of goodness as proof that Satan reigned supreme.

THE CALMING OF
THE STORM

And there arose a great storm of wind, and the waves beat into
the ship, so that it was now full. And he was in the hinder part
of the ship asleep on a pillow: and they awake him, and say unto
him, Master, carest thou not that we perish?

Mark 4:37-38

Perhaps just to escape from the crowds which thronged about him, or
perhaps to extend his work, Jesus decided to cross to the other side of
the Sea of Galilee. Touchingly, the account says that his fishermen
disciples 'took him even as he was' after they had sent away the multitude. It gives the
impression that Jesus was utterly spent; little wonder that he slept exhaustedly on the
high helmsman's seat in the stern of the boat.

Suddenly they found themselves caught in one of the sudden storms for which the
Sea of Galilee is notorious, and as the disciples struggled to save their boat from being
swamped they called urgently for Jesus to lend a hand. Waking, Jesus rebuked the wind
as if it were an unruly personal force, and commanded the sea to be still. The wind
ceased, the waves died away and they were floating peacefully in a great calm.

Clearly, the disciples had not expected a miracle, for the account ends with them
expressing fear and surprise. What kind of man was this, who could command the wind
and the sea?

The miracles where Jesus showed power over natural phenomena are often the most
difficult for a modern reader. For the Jewish disciples of Jesus and for the early
Christians this one would echo the story of the creation of the universe at the beginning
of the Book of Genesis. God created by stilling the chaotic storm of primeval forces and
separating light from darkness, heaven from earth and water from land. Day by day, the
process was extended until the whole creation was a single, ordered system in which
every aspect was good.

Whatever happened in the storm-tossed boat on the Sea of Galilee, his disciples
discovered that Jesus had powers similar to those which had brought the world into
existence. The experience made it easier for them to recognize that in everything he did
he aimed to turn chaos into order and evil into good.

76

THE GADARENE
SWINE

And the unclean spirits went out, and entered into the swine:
and the herd ran violently down a steep place into the sea (they
were about two thousand), and were choked in the sea.

Mark 5:13

Like so many of the incidents in the gospels, the story of the Gadarene
herd of pigs – which rushed to its end down a precipice into the Sea of
Galilee – has contributed a popular phrase to the English language.

In the original story, Jesus crossed the Sea of Galilee into a non-Jewish area called the
Decapolis, Greek for 'ten towns'. As the name suggests, the towns had long been
colonized by Greeks, and in AD1 they formed a trading and defensive federation against
local Jewish groups. The pigs mentioned in the incident would have been forbidden in
an area controlled by Jews because Hebrew law forbad eating pork.

The Decapolis was a foreign land to Jews, and for Jesus to go there indicated that he
intended to extend his teaching and healing work to Gentiles. But the story concentrates
on his encounter with a maniac suffering from multiple demonic possession and beyond
control even when chained.

Jesus ordered the evil spirits to reveal their name and then commanded them to leave
the man. By a strange kind of compassion he allowed them to enter a herd of pigs which
then rushed to their death in the lake. Understandably, the local people asked Jesus to go
away, and when the healed man asked to go with him Jesus told him to stay and tell
everyone about the miracle.

Jesus normally told people to keep his Messianic identity secret, but here there was
less danger of non-Jews thinking he had come as a political liberator. The story also
reveals a literal belief in demonic possession, and the need these evil spirits expressed to
inhabit some kind of living creature. It ends with Jesus returning immediately to Jewish
territory. If he had intended this to be a mission to foreigners, the encounter with the
maniac and his healing of him prevented him from doing anything further there.

THE SYNAGOGUE
PRESIDENT'S
DAUGHTER

While he yet spake, there came from the ruler of the synagogue's house certain which said, Thy daughter is dead: why troublest thou the Master any further? As soon as Jesus heard the word that was spoken, he saith unto the ruler of the synagogue, Be not afraid, only believe.

Mark 5:35-36

The gospels make it clear that they only contain some of the miracles that Jesus did, but these were carefully selected to indicate that he helped a wide range of people: Romans, Greeks and Jews, men and women, foreigners and Palestinians, young and old. It was important to show that his mission was free from nationalist, racist or even religious restrictions.

On returning to Galilee from the towns of the Decapolis, Jesus was met by a prominent Jew, president of a local synagogue. He fell at Jesus's feet and begged him to come and lay his hands on his small daughter, for she was at the point of death. Surrounded by a crowd, Jesus set out for the man's house.

On the way a woman approached him from behind and touched his cloak in the hope that the action might heal her. Whatever the nature of 'the issue of blood' from which she had suffered for twelve years, it made her ritually unclean. Although she had spent all she had on useless treatments, mere contact with Jesus's clothes cured her. Aware of what had happened, Jesus asked who had touched him. His disciples pointed out that a crowd was jostling him, but the woman came forward fearfully and Jesus told her that her faith had made her whole again.

The Raising of Jairus's Daughter by George Percy Jacomb-Hood (1857–1927), Guildhall Art Gallery, London.

The president of the synagogue at Capernaum asked Jesus to come and help his sick daughter, but on the way to the house he was told that she had died. Jesus went on in and raised her to life again.

Meanwhile, someone from the president's house arrived to say that his daughter had died and Jesus need not be troubled any further, but he went on into the house. There, despite their derision, Jesus assured the household that the girl was only sleeping; in his native Aramaic he told her to get up. She did so, and they were all so astonished that Jesus had to remind them to give her something to eat.

Was the girl really dead, or only in a deep coma? The derision of those present, and their subsequent astonishment suggest that she was indeed dead.

THE CHOICE OF THE APOSTLES

And he goeth up into a mountain, and calleth unto him whom he would: and they came unto him. And he ordained twelve, that they should be with him, and that he might send them forth to preach, and to have power to heal sicknesses, and to cast out devils.

Mark 3:13-15

Jesus attracted crowds of people who came to him for many different reasons: for help, to listen to him, to discredit him or to try to trap him into blasphemy or treason, and some just from curiosity. Of these many people, some attached themselves to him as disciples who travelled round with him to learn what they could from him. From these disciples Jesus chose twelve to form an inner group with special responsibilities.

The gospels refer to the members of this inner circle as 'apostles', a Greek word which means someone sent with delegated authority to perform a particular task. Their first duty was simply to be with Jesus, and this was the essential qualification the apostles eventually looked for when they had to replace Judas after he had hanged himself.

Mark says that Jesus also conferred on them his own Messianic powers to preach, heal and cast out devils. After the ascension of Jesus they would be the witnesses of his resurrection to the first Christians, and ensure that the New Testament writings were faithful to what Jesus himself had done and taught. Jesus himself left no record of his teachings, so all the information about him would depend on the twelve who had been with him from the beginning of his public ministry until its dramatic end in death, resurrection and ascension. Jesus promised them that the Holy Spirit would guide and strengthen them in their heavy responsibilities.

Remarkably, none of the twelve seem to have come from any of the groups with special training in Hebrew religious studies. The Palestine of Jesus's time abounded in such highly trained professionals as the scribes, and of priests centred on the Temple in Jerusalem, as well as such groups as Pharisees, Zealots and Essenes, each with its own distinctive expertise. Jesus seems to have ignored such people and to have turned to people from more humble trades and professions when choosing his apostles. After all, he himself had been brought up in the carpenter's workshop of an obscure northern village.

The Miraculous Draft of Fishes
Conrad Witz, Musée d'histoire et
d'art, Geneva.

Simon Peter and Andrew were two
of Jesus's first followers, and were
later chosen as his apostles.
Shortly after Jesus approached
them they caught a huge draft of
fishes, which they recognized as a
miracle.

Simon Peter (both names mean 'rock') and his brother Andrew were fishermen from
Bethsaida on the Sea of Galilee, who had also been disciples of John the Baptist. James
and John were also fishermen, and may have been cousins of Jesus. Peter, James and John
seem to have been closer to Jesus than the others.

Philip was also from Bethsaida, but his trade is not given. Matthew was a tax
collector in Capernaum, near Bethsaida. No mention is made of the home towns or
trades of Bartholomew or Thomas. James, son of Alphaeus, and Jude seem to have been
related to Jesus as close cousins or even brothers. Simon had been a member of the
Zealot party of Jewish nationalists at some time.

Judas Iscariot may have been the only apostle who did not come from Galilee if
'Iscariot' means someone from Kerioth in southern Judea, but it may be derived from
the Latin *sicarius* and mean 'dagger-man'. If so, Judas may have been an extremist who
expected Jesus to lead a Messianic freedom movement, but this is very conjectural.

Soon after their appointment as apostles Jesus sent the twelve out into the
countryside in pairs to preach. They were ordered to travel light with no money, and to
confine their missionary work to Jews, avoiding Gentile and Samaritan towns. He
warned them to expect opposition but to waste no time with people who did not
welcome them. They should be as wise as serpents but as harmless as doves.

These detailed instructions and warnings, given by Jesus to the apostles for their first
experience of working on their own, anticipate what they would later need as leaders of
the infant Christian church. Whatever their skills as fishermen, they would need
different skills as fishers of men.

THE MEMBERS OF THE KINGDOM OF HEAVEN

The kingdom of heaven is likened unto a man which sowed good seed in his field, but while men slept, his enemy came and sowed tares among the wheat, and went his way.

Matt 13:24-25

The kingdom of heaven' was one of the most characteristic phrases used by Jesus. Like so much of his teaching, he left the listeners to draw their own conclusions about the meaning; sometimes he offered a fuller explanation to his close disciples if they questioned him, but many scholars hold that these further comments were added later by the first Christians.

It might be taken for granted that the kingdom of heaven would be an ideal society in which every member put into practice the teaching of Jesus and showed perfect love towards all other people, whether friend or enemy. Two of the parables told by Jesus, the Tares in the Wheat and the Dragnet point to the reality.

In the the story of the Tares in the Wheat Jesus described a typical farming problem. A farmer and his labourers had sown a field with good seed, but as it grew it proved to be full of weeds very similar to the wheat. The farm workers asked the farmer of they should go into the wheat to weed it. No, he replied, leave the weeds in the wheat until the harvest when they could be separated without damaging the wheat.

In the other parable, Jesus turned to a fishing scene. A group of fishermen drew their net to the shore full of fish. There was no question of them trying to sort out the fish in the net while it was still in the sea, but once it was safely ashore they threw out the ones they did not want and kept the rest.

They are hard parables because they suggest that the members of the kingdom must tolerate dissidents and deviants, and leave the judgements to God in his own good time.

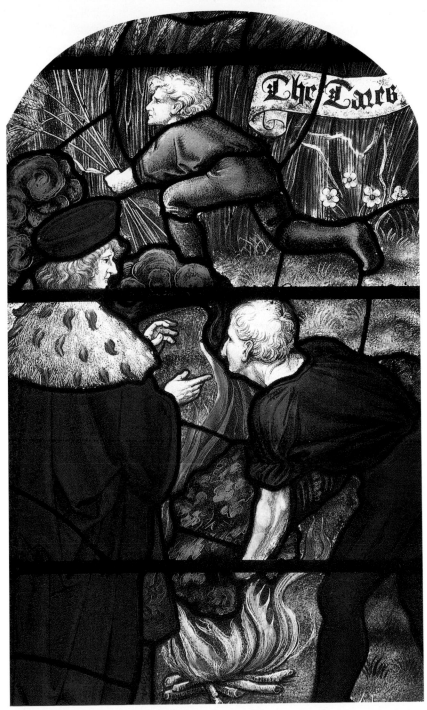

The Parable of the Tares
Hillesden Church, Bucks.

This 19th-century stained-glass window in an English parish church depicts a parable of judgement told by Jesus. The 'tares' are weeds growing in the wheat, but to weed them out before the harvest would damage the crop. The final judgement about who are worthy rests with God.

The kingdom of heaven is like to a grain of mustard seed, which a man took, and sowed in his field, which indeed is the least of all seeds: but when it is grown, it is the greatest among herbs, and becometh a tree, so that the birds of the air come and lodge in the branches thereof.

Matt 13:31-32

In several of his parables Jesus drew on the familiar experience of people who were prepared to take risks if they thought they might lead to wealth; the greater the possible wealth, the greater the risk they would take.

That pearls were much prized in the time of Jesus is shown by the story of the great pearl owned by Cleopatra of Egypt, which she dissolved in wine and drank to impress Mark Anthony. In the parable of the Pearl, Jesus told a story not of Cleopatra but of a pearl dealer who came across a particularly valuable pearl. He did not hesitate to risk selling everything he owned in order to buy the pearl. Jesus implied that the merchant would be able to gain far more profit from his pearl than all his previous wealth.

Similarly, in another parable, the Hidden Treasure, a man discovered a treasure buried in a field. He immediately buried it again and kept it secret until he had time to sell everything he owned so that he could buy the field. As in other parables told by Jesus, this one could be interpreted as encouraging injustice, or even theft, for it might be argued that the treasure belonged by right to the original owner of the field and he was being cheated of it. In parables there is only one, obvious point and other details are meant to be ignored.

The need for risk was never far from the surface in the teaching of Jesus and sometimes he made the point directly and in an extreme form to catch the attention of his listeners. He himself had risked losing the ordinary comforts and securities of life for the sake of his mission, and he told his followers that they must be prepared to take similar risks and make similar sacrifices if they wished to be members of his kingdom.

Some of the most unexpected points about membership of the kingdom of heaven were made by Jesus in parables of growth, sometimes with characteristic exaggeration. In the parable of the Mustard Seed, Jesus drew a contrast between the smallness of the seed and the great size of the tree which grows from it. The final outcome of the kingdom of heaven bears no relationship to its small beginnings.

To readers in more temperate climates familiar with mustard as a small salad plant or at best a wild shrub, the size of the tree in Jesus's story might seem poetic licence. He was referring, however, to a Palestinian tree, *brassica negra*, which grows to a considerable height and yields seeds which are ground to a fine powder for use as a spice. The contrast in the parable was between the powdered seed and the tree.

Another parable compared the growth of the kingdom of heaven with the effects of the yeast which a housewife kneads into the dough – the mixture of water and flour – to make 'leavened' bread. A very small amount of yeast will greatly increase the volume of the dough if it is left long enough to do its work. So too with the kingdom of heaven.

Exactly why the kingdom of heaven grows is beyond the knowledge of its members. In one parable Jesus compared its growth to seed which grew without anyone watching it. The seed was sown and the land then produced shoots, ears and full grain, apparently of its own accord day and night until harvest time. The kingdom of heaven has its own hidden powers.

Again, the kingdom of heaven is like unto a net, that was cast into the sea, and gathered of every kind, which, when it was full, they drew to shore, and sat down, and gathered the good into vessels, but cast the bad away.

Matt 13:47-48

THE MAN WITH THE WITHERED HAND

And he entered again into the synagogue; and there was there a man which had a withered hand. And they watched him, whether he would heal him on the sabbath day; that they might accuse him.

Mark 3:1-2

Nothing infuriated strictly legalistic Jews more than Jesus's attitude towards the sabbath, the day of rest ordered by Hebrew law for the last day of each week. Every person and every domestic animal had to cease work for 24 hours from sunset on Friday. This day of rest commemorated both the creation of the world, which God completed in six days and then rested, and the escape from Egypt, when God saved the Israelites from unremitting labour. It made everyone find time for worship as well as for rest.

Like all Hebrew laws, the basic sabbath law was attributed to the time when God dictated the law to Moses, and the practical applications were later elaborated in detailed regulations. The original intentions of the law were excellent, but problems arose when the letter of the regulations was applied uncompromisingly and the original spirit was lost.

As in all his treatment of law, Jesus cut through the letter to the underlying principle and behaved accordingly. He and his disciples were even accused of doing manual work when they munched ears of corn as they walked through cornfields on a sabbath. The Pharisees were not mollified by Jesus's retort that the sabbath was made for man, not man for the sabbath; the remark could be treated as blasphemy.

The last straw came when Jesus healed a man with a withered hand on a sabbath day in a synagogue. Not only did he heal him, but he pointedly asked whether it was better to allow the evil to continue because it was the sabbath, or to remove it. By now the enemies of Jesus were keeping a close watch on him. Infuriated by this latest provocation the Pharisees conferred with Herod's supporters, normally their political opponents, to see how they could destroy him.

THE FEEDING OF THE
FIVE THOUSAND

And when he had taken the five loaves and the two fishes, he looked up to heaven, and blessed, and brake the loaves, and gave them to his disciples to set before them; and the two fishes divided he among them all. And they did all eat, and were filled.

Mark 6:41-42

Thortly after they had heard about the murder of John the Baptist by Herod Antipas, Jesus and his disciples tried to get away to a remote place to escape from the crowds; but many people who knew them saw them going and followed after them, so Jesus preached to them. This is the setting for the story of the feeding of the five thousand.

When evening came and the crowds showed no sign of going, the disciples asked Jesus to send the people away to buy food for themselves, but Jesus told his disciples to get food for the crowd. They answered that food to the value of 200 days' wages would not be enough, so Jesus asked them what food there was. Philip answered, perhaps with some sarcasm, that there was a boy there with five small bread rolls and two fish. Jesus told them to organize the crowd into groups and get them to sit down.

Jesus then took the bread rolls and the fishes, raised his eyes to heaven in blessing, broke the food into pieces and gave them to the disciples to distribute to the crowd. All were filled, and there was enough left over to fill twelve baskets. The actions of Jesus were the same as the pattern of the communion meal, 'the breaking of bread', which quickly became the main form of worship for the first Christians and has remained so ever since.

The Feeding of the Five Thousand
Jacopo Bassano (c1519–1592),
Earl Spencer Collection, Althorp,
Northants.

Bassano sets this incident, Jesus's miraculous feeding of the crowd which
came to hear him teach, in his own Venetian countryside with people in
typical local costume, thus giving Jesus a local setting to emphasize his
modern relevance.

In John's gospel this is such a feature that the story of the miracle is followed by a
long report of a discussion next day between Jesus and some of the people who had been
present. Jesus accused them of following him because he could meet their material
needs; they must believe, he said, that he himself was the bread of life come down from
heaven.

As Jesus made increasingly extravagant claims for himself, the crowd faded away
until only his twelve closest disciples were left. Jesus asked them if they too were leaving
him. 'To whom shall we go?' answered Peter. 'Thou hast the words of eternal life.'

JESUS WALKS ON WATER

And when he had sent the multitudes away, he went up into a mountain apart to pray: and when the evening was come, he was there alone. But the ship was now in the midst of the sea, tossed with waves: for the wind was contrary. And in the fourth watch of the night Jesus went unto them, walking on the sea.

Matt. 14:23-25

The scene was very early morning, with Jesus on the western side of the Sea of Galilee and his disciples somewhere out on the waters. The previous evening Jesus had sent them across to Bethsaida while he stayed to placate a crowd which wanted to make him king. He had then used the rare moment of solitude for prayer.

As the first light touched the Sea of Galilee, Jesus saw the boat silhouetted against the dawn with the disciples still rowing hard against a contrary wind. Suddenly, as they faced away from the shore for their rowing, the disciples saw Jesus walking on the water alongside the boat. They screamed in terror, thinking it was an apparition, but Jesus reassured them.

When he realized it really was Jesus, Peter asked if he could join him on the water, and Jesus told him to come. Peter stepped over the side on to the water and began to walk, but his nerve failed and he began to sink. Jesus caught him, both of them climbed into the boat and the wind died away.

It is a strange event for a modern reader to accept, but the disciples' terror and Peter's impetuosity help to make it convincing. Some have suggested that it occurred in the period between the resurrection of Jesus and his ascension, when the gospels record similar incidents. But whenever it happened, it was more than a mere passing illusion caused by Jesus wading in shallow waters close inshore.

Jesus rebuked the disciples for their momentary terror, and reminded them about the recent miracle when he had fed five thousand. They should not have been surprised, he implied. Like the miracle when Jesus calmed the storm on the same stretch of water, the incident had echoes of the creation narrative at the beginning of the Book of Genesis. Even in the ordinary events of his ministry, the power available to Jesus was that of God the Creator rather than of a rabbi or teacher, even an outstandingly impressive one.

Jesus and Peter Walking on Water
Phillip Otto Runge (1777–1810)
Kunsthalle, Hamburg.

Strongly influenced by the literature of German romanticism and by Jakob Böhme, the German mystic, Runge depicts the incident when Peter stepped out of the boat to join Jesus walking on the water. Peter's faith failed him and Jesus had to hold him up.

89

THE TRADITION OF
THE ELDERS

And he called the multitude, and said unto them, Hear,
and understand: Not that which goeth into the mouth defileth
a man; but that which cometh out of the mouth, this
defileth a man.

Then came his disciples, and said unto him, Knowest thou
that the Pharisees were offended, after they heard this saying?

Matt. 15:10-12

In less than three years Jesus alienated every Hebrew group which thought it upheld the strict orthodoxy of the Hebrew religion, and this finally led to his arrest, condemnation and execution. His most angry confrontations were with the Pharisees, who were one of the most powerful of the ruling parties in the Sanhedrin, the Great Council of the Jews. By the time of Jesus they were the most conservative group in the Hebrew religion, and their very name meant that they were separated from other Jews by their rigid adherence to the letter of Hebrew law.

This particular confrontation began with an attack by Pharisees on Jesus and his disciples because they did not observe the complex ritual of washing prescribed by the law before eating a meal. From the beginning of his preaching work, Jesus had taught that it was more important to keep the spirit of the law than its letter, and in this confrontation he first rounded on the Pharisees for neglecting their family responsibilities under the guise of dedicating everything they possessed to the service of God.

90

Mosiac of Christ (detail)
South Gallery, Santa Sophia,
Istanbul, Turkey.

This 11th-century mosaic shows
Christ with his hand raised in an
attitude of blessing. The letters
either side of his head denote his
name, Jesus Christ.

Jesus then struck at the whole system of dietary laws. The law strictly forbade the
meat of any animals, such as pigs, which did not have cloven hoofs and chewed the cud.
Fish must have both fins and scales, so no shellfish were permitted. Jesus cut right across
all this by saying that people were not defiled by what went into their mouths but by
what they spoke, for words indicated attitudes. Where the words were evil, the heart was
evil also.

When the disciples warned Jesus that he had offended the Pharisees, he only went
further by saying that God would root up anything not planted by him, and that when
blind guides led the blind both fell into the pit. The blind guides were the Pharisees,
renowned for their strict observance of the religious traditions revealed by God to Moses.
Jesus's attitude would have appeared blasphemous to them.

THE MIRACLE AT THE
POOL

When Jesus saw him lie, and knew that he had been a long time in that case, he saith unto him, Wilt thou be made whole?

The impotent man answered him, Sir, I have no man, when the pool is troubled, to put me into the pool: but while I am coming, another steppeth down before me.

Jesus saith unto him, Rise, take up thy bed, and walk.

John 5:6-8

Jesus had gone to Jerusalem again for one of the main religious festivals - the gospel does not say which one - and this incident occurred at a pool fed by springs just north of the city's Temple area. The pool was surrounded by paving and walls, with five porches giving access to steps leading into the water. Its main function was to provide water for the Temple's needs, but the people believed that the water would cure the first person to be immersed in the pool whenever the water bubbled.

Like so many of the miracles Jesus performed, this one arose from an accidental encounter with someone who was exceptionally helpless. Among the jostling crowd by the pool lay a paralysed man who had no one to help him into the water when it stirred. He had no hope of being first, and so of being cured. Jesus was moved as much by his frustration as his illness, and simply told him to get up, take his bedding and walk. The man did so.

The account says nothing of the man's reaction to this unexpected miracle because he was immediately accused of breaking the law. It was a sabbath day, the seventh day of each week when all work was forbidden by Jewish law and he was caught carrying bedding. Moreover, he had done it almost in the Temple area itself, where the law would be strictly enforced. Jesus had gone, possibly to avoid the inevitable attention the miracle would attract, so the man could not tell his accusers who it was that had healed him.

Later in the day, Jesus came across the man in one of the public courtyards within the Temple complex, and he linked the cure with a more profound, spiritual healing. He told the man that he had been made whole, and should no more sin. Innocently, no doubt, the man went back to his accusers, who turned their anger on Jesus as a sabbath-breaker.

It is hard to believe that even the most fanatical members of the crowd which converged on Jesus in the Temple courtyards would seek to kill him for healing a man on the sabbath. Clearly, Jesus was already seen as a threat to religious tradition and the laws which guarded it; his remarks to this crowd demonstrated how well grounded their fears were.

Charged with sabbath-breaking, Jesus replied by claiming the same powers and privileges as God himself: 'My Father still goes on working, and I am at work, too.' The blasphemy could not have been clearer, and Jesus proceeded to elaborate it so that every Jew present would recognize what he was claiming. He not only claimed that he had the right, like God, to work whenever he wished, he further claimed that the Father had even shared with him the power to raise the dead to life again.

Jesus went on to use titles which in Jewish religious tradition could only apply to the Messiah himself. The time had already come, he said, when the dead would hear the voice of the Son of God, and would live as a consequence. Furthermore, Jesus continued, he had supreme judicial authority as Son of Man. Strangely enough, his claim to be 'Son of Man' was the greater blasphemy, because the Book of Daniel assigns this title to the heavenly being who will be sent by God at the end of world to judge all nations. Jesus's claim to this title would bring the death sentence on him at his trial.

Jesus hammered his claims home. He told his audience that they had asked John the Baptist about him, and John had told them the truth; but Jesus then told them that his own miracles were an even greater witness than John's testimony. If they refused to accept him after that kind of evidence it could only mean that they lacked God's love, Jesus continued, whatever Jewish history might say, and Moses himself would condemn them.

The hour is coming, and now is, when the dead shall hear the voice of the Son of God; and they that hear shall live. For as the Father hath life in himself; so hath he given to the Son to have life in himself; and hath given him authority to execute judgement also, because he is the Son of man.

John 5:25-27

THE WOMAN TAKEN
IN ADULTERY

He that is without sin among you, let him first cast a stone at her. And they which heard it, being convicted by their own conscience, went out one by one, beginning at the eldest, even unto the last: and Jesus was left alone, and the woman standing in the midst.

John 8:7-8

Soon Jesus returned to Galilee to consolidate his main missionary base there, and then went to Jerusalem again for the Feast of Tabernacles, the last of the three great harvest festivals in the Jewish religious calendar. He spent much of his time in the public courtyards of the Temple area and his reputation was such that many gathered to listen to him.

While he was surrounded by the crowd, representatives of the scribes and Pharisees tried to trap him with a legal case. An unfortunate married woman had been caught in the act of adultery, sexual intercourse with a man who was not her husband. Hebrew law prescribed the death penalty by stoning, and the witnesses whose evidence had led to the conviction were required to start the execution by throwing the first stones.

The woman's accusers and judges asked Jesus what he thought they should do. Whatever he answered could be used to discredit him with the crowd; he would either appear to be condoning the offence in contempt of the Mosaic law, or appear to be approving of the woman's execution. In fact, the Roman administration did not allow the Jewish authorities to carry out executions, but that did not lessen the problem for Jesus.

The Woman Taken in Adultery
(bottom left)
St. Pierre, Dreux, France.

Part of a 16th-century stained-
glass window depicting four
scenes from the life of Christ.
Jesus was asked to judge a woman
caught in adultery. Writing in the
sand in parody of a written
judgement, he invited any sinless
person present to cast the first
stone. No one did.

Instead of committing himself to an answer, Jesus asked them whether their own consciences allowed them to make such a judgement about the woman and carry out the sentence. By giving this answer, Jesus transformed the case from a legal issue into a moral question, and none of the woman's accusers were prepared to press it to its legal conclusion.

One by one, the accusers left the scene until only the woman remained. In one of the most poignant exchanges in the gospels, Jesus asked her if anyone remained to condemn her. She replied that there was none. Jesus told her that neither did he; she should go, and sin no more.

The absence of this passage from the earliest manuscripts suggests that it was inserted into John's Gospel by someone other than the gospel's original author. This need not mean that the incident did not happen, and it is entirely consistent with Jesus's compassion and his attitude towards people who tried to embarrass him.

THE LIGHT OF THE WORLD

In the beginning was the Word, and the Word was with God, and the Word was God. In him was life, and the life was the light of men. And the light shineth in darkness; and the darkness comprehended it not ...

John 1:1-3

The Light of the World
William Holman Hunt
(1827–1910), Keble College,
Oxford (right).

The famous picture was inspired by Jesus's claim, 'I am the light of the world,' and depicts him knocking at a long-closed door symbolizing the human soul. The words painted on the frame, 'Behold, I stand at the door, and knock ...', are from the New Testament Book of the Revelation of St. John the Divine.

When Jesus told the Pharisees that he was the light of the world, he was speaking in the Temple area of Jerusalem during the Feast of Tabernacles. This great harvest festival was held in the autumn at the end of the agricultural year when the people built temporary shelters (tabernacles) in the fields to get in the last of their crops before the winter rains started.

Lights played an important role in the celebrations. A great candelabra was lit in one of the Temple courtyards, and every home had lamps burning throughout the feast. They symbolized the pillar of fire which led the people during their escape from Egypt, the prosperity God gave his people in the promised land, and the light shed by God's law. In these surroundings, Jesus claimed that he was the light of the world. To his audience, it was an unmistakeable assertion that he thought he was God, and the Pharisees naturally challenged him; but he had the sympathy of the crowd and for the time being the religious authorities made no move to stop him.

But Jesus went on to challenge the ordinary Jews as well, because they thought that mere descent from Abraham guaranteed them the privileges of God's promises. Abraham was the first Hebrew to receive a covenant from God, and all Jews traced their descent from him.

In a cryptic remark, Jesus told his audience that Abraham had been glad to see Jesus's day. Mockingly, they riposted that Jesus was not yet 50; how could he have seen

Then spake Jesus
again unto them,
saying, I am the
light of the world:
he that followeth
me shall not walk
in darkness, but
shall have the light
of life.

John 8:12

Abraham? Jesus replied that he was already alive before Abraham was born. At this the crowd lost its patience with his claims and took up stones to stone him. Jesus hurriedly left.

Such uncompromising claims for himself would eventually cost Jesus his life when the authorities judged that it was safe to arrest him, but he was not prepared to compromise in his teaching even if it alienated the ordinary people.

THE MAN BORN BLIND

Then again called they the man that was blind, and said unto him, Give God the praise: we know that this man is a sinner. He answered and said, Whether he be a sinner or no, I know not: one thing I know, that, whereas I was blind, now I see.

John 9:24-28

Once again, an accidental encounter with Jesus led to a miracle of healing, this time of a man by the side of the road, who had been blind from birth. Jesus noticed him as he passed. But the gospel account gives less space to the miracle than to the consequences of it, when the healed man was cross-examined by the local religious leaders in an attempt to discredit Jesus.

They refused to believe that the man really had been born blind or that he was the same man. The authorities had already ruled that anyone who said Jesus was the Messiah would be excommunicated from the local synagogue. That meant ruin; they would be excluded from their own community. The man's parents were frightened. 'He is of age,' they said when questioned, 'ask him.'

So the Pharisees cross-examined the man himself about Jesus, but they could get nowhere; he merely described what had happened and said that Jesus was a prophet. They then bluntly asserted that they knew that Jesus was a sinner, but the man would only say that he knew he had been blind and he knew that he could now see.

They pressed him further, only looking for something to discredit Jesus, until the man rounded on them: 'Since the world began it was not heard that any man opened the eyes of one that was born blind. If this man were not of God, he could do nothing.' So they excommunicated him. Later, Jesus revealed to the man who he was. Then he said it was the blind who could really see, and those with sight who were blind. Some Pharisees asked him if they too were blind. If they thought they could see, said Jesus, they remained unforgiven.

THE GOOD SHEPHERD

I am the good shepherd, and know my sheep and am known of mine. As the Father knoweth me, even so know I the Father: and I lay down my life for the sheep. And other sheep I have, which are not of this fold: them also I must bring, and they shall hear my voice; and there shall be one fold, and one shepherd.

John 10:14-16

The third of the visits made by Jesus to Jerusalem during his adult ministry was for the annual festival of the Dedication of the Temple. Although it was not one of the great pilgrimage feasts, the Dedication was one of the most popular ones, as it celebrated the rededication of the Temple by Judas Maccabaeus in 164BC. The event had marked the triumphal end of three years of bitter warfare against the Greek emperors who had controlled Palestine and defiled the Temple.

The nationalist feelings expressed by this festival were an appropriate background for Jesus's teaching about the qualities of a shepherd. The Hebrew people were familiar with the allegory of their rulers as shepherds, as it featured prominently in the prophetic denunciations of corrupt Hebrew kings.

David, the greatest of all Hebrew kings, had been a shepherd when he was chosen and elected as the first effective king, and the Hebrew people themselves were nomadic shepherds during the centuries before their occupation of Palestine.

In his teaching, Jesus laid stress on the relationship of the shepherd to his sheep, for the good shepherd could identify all of his sheep by name and lead them. Most significantly, the good shepherd was prepared to die in defence of his sheep. Jesus identified himself as the good shepherd, who was not only prepared to die for his sheep, but also to bring them life.

There was a sharp contrast between the ideal shepherd described by Jesus, and the attitudes of the people's religious leaders. By this stage of his ministry, Jesus had had

Feed my Sheep
Stained glass, Streatham.

Jesus applied the image of a good
shepherd to himself and his work.
Consequently it was also the
central theme of what he said
when he delegated responsibility
to his disciples, particularly Peter.
They were to feed his sheep.

ample experience of the suspicion and opposition his actions and teaching aroused in the
nation's official religious leaders, who resented anything which they thought might be a
threat to their power. His mention of 'other sheep, which are not of this fold' also
pointed to the universalism of his teaching, compared with the narrow and exclusive
nationalism of official Hebrew religious teaching in his time.

100

The Month of May: Christ as the Good Shepherd
Abel Grimmer (*c*1570–*c*1619), private collection.

The Reformation caused a decline in religious paintings for churches in the Netherlands, but religious elements still appeared in secular paintings. The halo and sumptuous robes identify the shepherd as Jesus in this painting of the month of May.

THE CANAANITE
WOMAN

Then came she and worshipped him, saying, Lord, help me. But
he answered and said, It is not meet to take the children's bread,
and to cast it to dogs. And she said, Truth, Lord: yet the dogs
eat of the crumbs which fall from their masters' table.

Matt. 15:25-27

efore he started out on his last journey to Jerusalem, Jesus withdrew
from Jewish territory into the Lebanon. He tried to keep his visit secret,
but word of his presence spread quickly and a woman from near Tyre
came to the house where he was staying to ask help for her sick daughter.

The gospels do not record many encounters between Jesus and Gentiles, and in this
case the woman had a frosty reception both from the disciples and from Jesus. The
disciples urged Jesus to send her away because she was shouting at them, and Jesus
seemed to agree, for he said that his mission was only to 'the lost sheep of the house of
Israel'.

But the woman was desperate. She finally gained access to Jesus, prostrated herself
before him and asked for his help. Jesus told her that it was not right to throw the
children's food to dogs. Despite the rebuff, the woman replied that the dogs could eat
any crumbs which had fallen from the table.

She had turned the rebuff into a means of expressing her faith in Jesus and her
willingness to accept any insult for the sake of her daughter. Moved by her persistence,
Jesus told her that she had great faith, and that her daughter was healed, as indeed she
found when she returned home.

The incident is reminiscent of the healing of the Centurion's servant, where Jesus
drew such a strong contrast between the faith of Gentiles and Jews. But this present
exchange emphasized that he tried to confine his attention to his fellow Jews, where he
could build on Hebrew religious traditions which had evolved over so many centuries.

The first generation of Christians would have to tackle the problem of how to relate
Hebrew tradition and the teaching of Jesus to Gentiles who wanted to be Christians.
Jesus did show that he could accept and help anyone who had faith, whatever their
nationality, but in the brief time available his first priority was to teach his fellow Jews,
and particularly his disciples.

THE HEALING
OF THE DEAF-MUTE

And straightway his ears were opened, and the string of his tongue was loosed, and he spake plain. And he charged them that they should tell no man: but the more he charged them, so much the more a great deal they published it.

Mark 7:35-36

The number of places in the north of Palestine Jesus visited during this period of his ministry shows that he and his disciples were constantly on the move. By now his main concern was to instruct his disciples, but he was increasingly hindered by the crowds which sought him out wherever he went.

One such crowd containing many sick people followed him into the hills above the Sea of Galilee, where a deaf-mute was brought to him. Jesus took him to one side and healed him by putting spittle on his tongue and using the command 'be opened'.

As on other occasions, Jesus told the man and his friends to keep quiet about the cure, but they told everyone. Others in need pressed forward and were healed, and the crowd was overwhelmed by the wonder of it all.

Jesus was aware of the dangers in this kind of adulation, particularly as northern Galilee was notorious for its armed resistance movements. The crowd could easily think he was the invincible 'Son of David', the Messianic hero whom God would send to liberate them, and expect Jesus to lead an armed rebellion against the Roman occupation. At this stage of his plans it was essential for Jesus to avoid the crisis such a move would provoke.

The incident led to another miraculous feeding of a crowd in a remote place, four thousand people this time. Many commentators suggest that this story is a duplicate of the earlier feeding of the five thousand, but there are differences which leave it an open question. Whether or not this was another feeding miracle, the crowd in this account was largely composed not of Jews but of Gentiles, and Jesus was as willing to help them as he was his own nationality.

As on other occasions, Jesus and his disciples only got away from the crowds again by taking to a boat.

PETER'S ACCEPTANCE OF JESUS AS MESSIAH

And I say unto thee, That thou art Peter, and upon this rock I will build my church; and the gates of hell shall not prevail against it. And I will give unto thee the keys of the kingdom of heaven: and whatsoever thou shalt bind on earth shall be bound in heaven: and whatsoever thou shalt loose on earth shall be loosed in heaven.

Matt. 16:18-19

Jesus had been teaching for two years. He must by now have realized that he would attract crowds wherever he went and that he could not control their crude Messianic expectations. He and the disciples were at Caesarea Philippi, the most northern town in Jewish territory at the foot of Mount Hermon. He began to make plans for the final journey to Jerusalem which would culminate in his death.

The disciples had been with Jesus for two years and had seen what he did and heard what he preached. His private instruction of them had reached the point where they were beginning to accept him on his own terms and to realize that he gave a different meaning to the traditional beliefs of Hebrew religion.

Jesus asked the disciples what people were saying about him. Who did they think he was? They replied that some thought he was John the Baptist, who had been executed; some thought he was Elijah, who would return according to popular tradition to prepare the way for the Messiah; and some thought he was a prophet as great as Jeremiah.

Then Jesus asked them what they themselves thought about him. Peter replied that he was the Messiah (the gospels, written in Greek, use 'Christ', the Greek translation of the Hebrew word 'Messiah'). Jesus told Peter that this was no mere human deduction but a revelation from God.

Jesus went on to make a pun on the names Simon Peter, both of which mean 'rock'. He would build his church on this rock, he said, and not even the forces of hell would be able to destroy it. Moreover, Peter would be given the keys of the kingdom of heaven, and heaven would honour the judgements he made.

There has been endless debate about the meaning of these words of Jesus to Peter, and even bloodshed, throughout the history of Christianity. Whatever their meaning, Peter himself would very soon learn that he could still earn sharp rebukes from Jesus for being mistaken.

CHRIST'S FIRST PREDICTION OF HIS DEATH

From that time forth began Jesus to show unto his disciples, how he must go unto Jerusalem, and suffer many things of the elders and chief priests and scribes, and be killed, and be raised again the third day.

Matt. 16:21

Once the disciples had acknowledged Jesus as Messiah on something like his own terms, Jesus could begin to expand the explanations he gave them. So far there had been no suggestion from Jesus that his mission might soon end in his death, but now he told them it would.

Jesus and his disciples were at the most northern place in Jewish territory; now he told them that they must begin to make their way down through Galilee and the valley of the River Jordan to Judaea and Jerusalem. It would be a journey of about 150 miles. Once there, he warned them, he would be rejected, maltreated by the nation's religious leaders and executed.

He would not need any divine or even prophetic gifts to foresee such an outcome. Jesus had been to Jerusalem several times before, and had run into trouble there because of the things he said and did. So far he had discouraged any popular recognition that he was the Messiah. This time he intended to enter Jerusalem with his disciples in a manner which invited popular acclamation and challenged the religious authorities at their centre of power.

It was inevitable that the crowds would quickly reject him when they realized he was not their kind of Messiah, and the Great Council of the Jews would certainly condemn him for blasphemy. They would then have little problem in bringing him before the Roman governor on a capital charge, and he would be executed by crucifixion, the normal method for a person without privileges.

Peter protested vehemently to Jesus, as well he might, so Jesus called him 'Satan' – God's agent for testing his people's faith – and told him that he was still thinking by human standards instead of the way Jesus had taught him. Twice more on the journey Jesus tried to explain to his disciples what would be happening, but with little success.

THE
TRANSFIGURATION
OF CHRIST

And after six days Jesus taketh Peter, James, and John his
brother, and bringeth them up into a high mountain apart, and
was transfigured before them: and his face did shine as the sun,
and his raiment was white as the light. And behold there
appeared unto them Moses and Elijah talking with him.

Matt. 17:1-3

The Transfiguration is one of the strangest incidents in the whole story of Jesus Christ. Shortly after his decision to travel with his disciples to Jerusalem to bring his ministry to its climax, Jesus took the three leading disciples onto a mountain and for a brief period was transformed in front of them. His face and his garments shone with a brilliant light, and two figures identified as Moses and Elijah appeared and spoke with him.

Peter offered to make three shelters for Jesus and his two visitors, but a bright cloud descended on them all, and a voice from the cloud said, 'This is my beloved Son, in whom I am well pleased; hear ye him.' The disciples threw themselves on the ground in terror, but Jesus came and touched them, and told them to get up and not to be afraid. They got up, and when they looked around Jesus was alone again.

The apparitions and the voice pointed to the significance of what had happened. The four books of the Old Testament from Exodus to Deuteronomy record that Moses received the most important and extensive revelation from God in all Hebrew tradition,

when God dictated the Law to him. That revelation began on the top of a mountain clothed in a bright cloud. Jesus was the new, the greater Moses.

Elijah was the first of the long line of Hebrew prophets, inspired by God, who taught that God would send his Messiah to complete the whole plan of salvation. Jesus was the fulfilment of all those prophecies.

The voice from the cloud linked this event with the baptism of Jesus, when a similar voice proclaimed him the beloved Son of God in words which similarly echoed the coronation formula for Hebrew kings.

The whole incident gave the final journey to Jerusalem a divine context. It would not be a futile quest by the leader of a lost cause, but the final triumph of God's saving power over everything which tried to thwart it.

The Transfiguration
Church of Daphni Monastery, Greece.

The 11th-century mosaic depicts an incident near the beginning of the last journey of Jesus and his disciples to Jerusalem. Jesus took three of them to a mountain top where they saw him bathed in light and talking with Moses and Elijah. A voice proclaimed him 'my beloved Son' and told them to listen to him.

107

THE HEALING OF AN EPILEPTIC BOY

A man of the company cried out, saying, Master, I beseech thee, look upon my son: for he is mine only child. And lo, a spirit taketh him, and he suddenly crieth out; and it teareth him that he foameth again, and bruising him hardly departeth from him. And I besought thy disciples to cast him out; and they could not.

Luke 9:38-39

Jesus and the three disciples closest to him descended from the Mount of Transfiguration to a scene of chaos. The remaining disciples had been surrounded by a crowd of sick people and their friends, all looking for help from Jesus, and the disciples had been able to do nothing for them. As Jesus approached, a man ran up to him with a desperate plea for his epileptic son. He had pleaded with the disciples to heal him, but they had proved to be useless.

The man now urged Jesus that if he could do anything, he should help him and the boy. Indignantly, Jesus echoed the man's words: 'If he could!' and he asked him if he had faith. The man replied that he did have, but it was insufficient, and asked Jesus to help him in his lack of faith. Jesus did so, quickly and directly, by healing the boy.

In the course of the incident, Jesus had some harsh things to say to his disciples. They and the crowd were a faithless generation, he said, and he asked them pointedly how long they thought he would be with them to help; how long, indeed, would he have to tolerate them! The kind of spirit possessing the boy, he continued, could only be

Christ Blessing Little Children
Warwick Brookes (1808–1882),
Victoria and Albert Museum,
London.

When children were brought
before Jesus to be touched by him,
the disciples rebuked those who
brought them, thinking that Jesus
had other work to do. But Jesus
welcomed the children and
blessed them.

defeated by fasting and prayer. The rebuke to those surrounding Jesus was explicit. Such evil as gripped the boy could only be met by the discipline of self-restraint and commitment to God; it was not surprising that they had failed.

The gospel account says that the fit left the boy apparently dead, and Jesus raised him up. This kind of language shows that the incident has been selected and placed within the structure of the gospel narrative to point towards Jesus's own approaching death and resurrection, and the unique quality of his commitment to God. Evil could be overcome, but only by the kind of total faith Jesus possessed.

THE GOOD
SAMARITAN

But a certain Samaritan, as he journeyed, came where he was:
and when he saw him, he had compassion on him, and went to
him, and bound up his wounds, pouring in oil and wine, and set
him on his own beast, and brought him to an inn, and took care
of him.

Luke 10:33-34

The parable of the Good Samaritan must be one of the best-known of all stories, for anyone who helps the distressed is a 'Samaritan'. Jesus told it vividly. A traveller on the notoriously dangerous road from Jerusalem to Jericho was attacked by thieves who left him stripped and wounded by the roadside. A Hebrew priest and a Levite saw the injured man but passed by without helping him. Eventually a Samaritan arrived on the scene, tended the man's wounds, got him to an inn and took care of all expenses until he was restored to health.

The characters in the story represented clearly-defined groups in Hebrew society: the exclusive, inherited priesthood which presided at all Temple services; the Levite officials responsible for running the complex administration of the Temple and the system of taxation which financed it; and the Samaritans.

Samaritans took their name from Samaria, the large region of Palestine between Judaea and Galilee. Its Hebrew tribes had successfully rebelled against rule from Jerusalem at the death of King Solomon, its population had been deported by foreign conquerors and replaced, and soldiers of many victorious armies had settled in it. The

The Parable of the Good Samaritan
St. John's Church, Rownhams,
Hampshire.

The 16th-century Flemish stained-glass roundel shows the Samaritan
helping the wounded traveller. A man with a staff of office and a mitred
bishop reading a book have passed by. At the time when Jesus told the
story orthodox Jews despised Samaritans.

Samaritans even had their own religious centres and ignored the Temple in Jerusalem.
Jesus's choice of a Samaritan as the hero of his parable was a thrust at the prejudices of all
orthodox Jews.

Parables pose questions for the listeners to answer. In this case a specialist in Hebrew
religious law gave the correct answers in response to Jesus's story. The lawyer had first
asked how to obtain eternal life; Jesus had asked him in return what Hebrew law had to
say and the lawyer replied with the law's summaries about love. Jesus congratulated
him. The lawyer then asked for more detailed guidance, so Jesus told him the famous
story. Again he gave the answer Jesus wanted. Eternal life belonged to those who behave
like the Samaritan; in doing so they fulfilled the law.

DENUNCIATIONS OF
RELIGIOUS LEADERS

Woe unto you also, ye lawyers! for ye lade men with burdens grievous to be borne, and ye yourselves touch not the burdens with one of your fingers. Woe unto you! for ye build sepulchres of the prophets, and your fathers killed them.

Luke 11:46-47

Once again Jesus encountered criticism of his own religious commitment because he did not observe all the details of the complex Hebrew religious laws regulating food and eating. He had accepted a Pharisee's invitation to a meal, and his host had rebuked him even before the meal began. The gospel account makes it clear that many other people were present.

Jesus in turn rebuked his host and his Pharisee colleagues for meticulously keeping the details of the law while failing to observe its spirit. It was the message which Jesus had recently given in the parable of the Good Samaritan; only those who kept the spirit of the law could expect approval from God.

The Pharisees, said Jesus, counted the very leaves of their herbs to give the exact tenth required by the law, but failed to show justice or the love of God. They expected to be honoured as particularly devout people, Jesus continued, but in reality they were like hidden graves which defiled anyone who trod on them.

One of the lawyers present asked Jesus if he included them in his strictures. Originally responsible for making accurate copies of the ancient Mosaic law, the lawyers had become official exponents of its application to new circumstances. Their leaders were members of the Sanhedrin, the Great Council of Judaism.

Jesus replied that he did indeed include them in his condemnations, because they enforced every detail of the law instead of helping people to observe the principles it enshrined. They built elaborate tombs for the prophets as a mark of their respect, he continued, but the prophets had been killed because they denounced the very legalism the lawyers still practised.

Jesus ended his tirade by accusing his fellow guests of taking away the key of knowledge, the religious and moral principles underlying the law. They themselves had failed to enter into the real knowledge of God, and they hindered others from doing so.

CHRIST AGAIN PREDICTS HIS DEATH

They said unto him, Grant unto us that we may sit, one on thy right hand, and the other on thy left hand, in thy glory.

But Jesus said unto them, Ye know not what ye ask: can ye drink of the cup that I drink of? and be baptized with the baptism that I am baptized with?'

Mark 10:37-38

Before they set out on their last journey, Jesus had given the disciples their first clear warning of what awaited him in Jerusalem. He repeated the warnings twice again in the course of the journey: he would be betrayed, tortured and crucified, and after three days he would rise again.

The idea that he would rise again from death made little impact on them. Peter had protested strongly when Jesus first told them, and Jesus had rebuked him for it. They all reacted with baffled silence the second time he told them, and were afraid to ask him what he meant. On the third occasion two of the disciples, James and John, asked Jesus if he would make them the most important people in his kingdom when he came into his glory.

Startled by their request, Jesus retorted that they did not realize what they were asking. Were they able to withstand the ordeal he was facing, he asked? To drink the cup he would drink and the overwhelming dereliction with which he was to be baptized? They innocently said that they were able to. Their reply showed that they had no inkling of what Jesus was warning them about.

Sadly, Jesus told them that they would indeed go through comparable experiences before they were finished, but he did not have the power to assign places of importance. It was a gentle way of closing the incident.

But the other disciples were angry that two of their number should try to gain special privileges from Jesus, and they would not let the matter rest. Jesus called them all to him and told them, as he had earlier told Peter, that they were thinking the way the world thinks. Secular kingdoms had hierarchies of authority and privilege, he said, but they must not imitate such systems. In his kingdom the leaders must be the servants of all and the last to be honoured. Like himself, the Son of Man, Jesus told them, they must be prepared to give their lives for the many.

THE PRODIGAL SON

I will arise and go to my father, and will say unto him, Father, I have sinned against heaven, and before thee, and am no more worthy to be called thy son: make me as one of thy hired servants.

Luke 15:18-19

During his last journey to Jerusalem, Jesus told some of his most biting parables to emphasize God's love for outcasts, and to rebuke religious leaders who criticized him for mixing with people rejected by conventional society.

Jesus reminded them of what people actually did when they lost something. If a shepherd with 100 sheep lost one of them, he went looking for it until he had found it. If a woman mislaid a sum of money, she swept the house and searched for it. Both of them shared their delight with their friends when they found what they had lost. God, said Jesus, was like that about sinners, and there was similar rejoicing in heaven when one of them repented.

The third parable with which Jesus made this point was one of his most delightful, the Lost, or 'Prodigal' Son. Jesus told the story of a younger son who claimed his inheritance and moved to another country. While his money lasted he was surrounded by new friends, but once it had gone they all deserted him.

The boy obtained employment as a swineherd, but became so hungry and desperate that he decided to return humbly to his father, tell him how foolishly sinful he had been

The Parable of the Prodigal Son
Burlinson and Gryles', Hillesden
Church, Bucks.

The two stained-glass windows of 1875 depict the spendthrift boy of the
parable in misery as a swineherd after he had wasted his inheritance, and
being welcomed rapturously by his father when he returned home
penitent.

and ask to be employed as a labourer. But as soon as he came into sight his father rushed
to welcome him. The boy duly made his speech of penitence, but the father feted him
and 'killed the fatted calf' for him.

The rejoicing was only marred by the elder brother's anger when he arrived home
from work in the fields. He complained to his father that he had always been faithful
and obedient, but he had never been given so much as a kid to make merry with his
friends. The father reminded him that he would inherit everything, but these festivities
were for a son who had returned from the dead.

Parables usually only have one point, and in this it is the welcome God gives to the
penitent, but Jesus might also have hoped that some of his Jewish audience would
recognize themselves in the elder brother.

The Parable of the Prodigal Son
The Master of the Female Half
Lengths, Christie's, London.

The anonymous 16th-century
artist has set the parable in a small
German town of his own times.
The younger son is seen claiming
his heritage at the town gate,
squandering it lavishly while a
jester watches, being thrown out
of an inn when all was spent, and
living as a lonely swineherd.

SUFFER LITTLE
CHILDREN

They brought unto him also infants, that he would touch them:
but when his disciples saw it, they rebuked them. But Jesus
called them unto him, and said, Suffer little children to come
unto me, and forbid them not: for of such is the kingdom of God.

Luke 18:15-16

It was a touching scene, easily romanticized. Some parents pressed forward with young children for Jesus to touch, but the disciples tried to prevent them. Jesus was indignant with his disciples, and told them to allow the children to come to him. Taking the children in his arms, Jesus blessed them, and said that only those who were prepared to become like little children would be able to enter the kingdom of God.

It was customary for parents to bring their children to be blessed by the scribes on the Day of Atonement, and the disciples may have resented any comparison between Jesus and a class of official he had so often criticized. Possibly, they were only trying to protect Jesus when they thought he was occupied with more important matters. But Jesus's indignation indicates that an important principle was at stake. He told the disciples and the crowd that their salvation depended on turning from their adult attitudes to become children again.

The gospels report other similar remarks by Jesus. Anyone who made himself as insignificant as a child, he said, would be the greatest in the kingdom of heaven. Anyone who welcomed a child in his name, he added, welcomed Jesus himself. And most

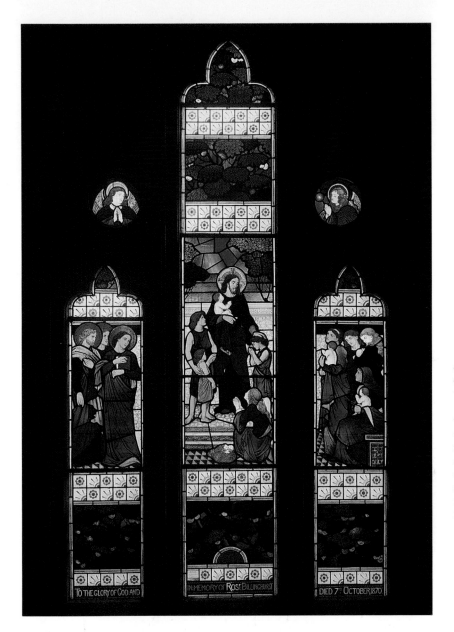

Christ Blessing The Children
G.E. Cook, Cricklade Church,
Wiltshire.

This stained-glass memorial
window of 1875 depicts Jesus
blessing children after his
desciples had tried to prevent
them from troubling him. Jesus
said that only those who become
like little children could enter the
Kingdom of Heaven.

significantly, anyone who caused the downfall of a child who had faith in him would be
better drowned in the depths of the sea with a millstone round his neck.

These sayings show that Jesus was pointing to the simple trust children give to an
adult when they are in need of anything. This was the model for the faith in God
required for entry into God's realm of salvation. The incident was immediately followed
by the rich and devout young man who asked Jesus what he should do to obtain eternal
life. Jesus told him to sell everything, give the proceeds to the poor, and come with him;
but it was too much to ask.

BLIND BARTIMAEUS, AND ZACCHAEUS

As he went out of Jericho with his disciples and a great number of people, blind Bartimaeus, the son of Timaeus, sat by the highway side begging. And when he heard that it was Jesus of Nazareth, he began to cry out, and say, Jesus, thou Son of David, have mercy on me.

Mark 10:46-47

Christ's Entry into Jerusalem
Burghley House, Stamford, Lincolnshire (right).

This early 16th-century painting of the Netherlandish School depicts Jesus in the last stage of his journey through Jericho to Jerusalem. The man in the tree recalls Zacchaeus, the tax-collector of Jericho, who climbed a tree in order to see Jesus and became a follower of him.

Jericho, at the southern end of the of the River Jordan's deep valley, was the final stop for Jesus on his way to Jerusalem for the last Passover of his life. As he and the disciples were passing through the oasis city on the barren shores of the Dead Sea, a blind beggar named Bartimaeus shouted out to him and hailed him as Son of David, a popular title for the Messiah.

Those around tried to quieten him, but Bartimaeus only shouted the Messianic title more loudly, together with a plea for pity. Jesus stopped and told the people around to bring Bartimaeus to him, so Bartimaeus threw off his cloak and went to him. Jesus asked him what he wanted him to do for him. Bartimaeus addressed Jesus as 'my master' and asked him to let him see again. Jesus told him to go, and that his faith had saved him. His sight returned immediately, and he followed Jesus along the road.

A further incident in Jericho had its humorous aspect. As so often happened, a crowd surrounded Jesus as he moved along, and a short tax collector named Zacchaeus darted about the edge of the crowd trying to catch a glimpse of the famous teacher. In the end he ran ahead and climbed into a tree. Looking up and seeing him, Jesus called to him to

And when Jesus came to the place, he looked up, and saw him, and said unto him, Zacchaeus, make haste, and come down; for to day I must abide at thy house.

Luke 19:5

come down because he wished to lodge in his house. Zacchaeus happily complied.

As a businessman who collected taxes for the profit he could make, Zacchaeus practised a notoriously corrupt profession, and Jesus was again criticized for befriending such a person. But Zacchaeus volunteered to give half of his wealth to the poor and to restore four times the amount of any tax money he had taken unjustly. Jesus told him that salvation had come to his house that day, and that the Son of Man came to search out and save what was lost.

THE RAISING OF
LAZARUS

He cried with a loud voice, Lazarus, come forth. And he that
was dead came forth, bound hand and foot with grave clothes:
and his face was bound with a napkin. Jesus saith unto them,
Loose him, and let him go.

John 11:43-44

The village of Bethany was two miles from Jerusalem on the road from
Jericho, so Jesus and the disciples would have to pass through it. Three
close friends of Jesus lived there, the sisters Martha and Mary, and their
brother Lazarus. As Jesus and the disciples reached Jericho on their journey along the
valley of the River Jordan, they received news that Lazarus was ill.

Jesus waited two days in Jericho before he made any move, and then he told the
disciples that he was going to Bethany even though Lazarus had by now died. The
disciples were worried about the danger faced by Jesus so near Jerusalem but they were
resigned to going 'that we may die with him'. By the time they reached Bethany Lazarus
had been buried for four days.

Martha went to meet Jesus, and told him that if he had been there Lazarus would not
have died. Jesus replied that Lazarus would rise again, and when Martha thought he
meant the final resurrection of everyone, he said, 'I am the resurrection and the life.'
Martha told him that she believed he was the Messiah, the Son of God.

Jesus, the two sisters and a number of mourners all went to the tomb, a cave with a
stone across the opening. Jesus wept, and told them to remove the stone. They protested

The Raising of Lazarus
Sebastiano del Piombo
(c 1485–1547), National Gallery,
London.

Originally painted for Narbonne
Cathedral, Piombo's illustration of
the raising of Lazarus shows the
influence of Michelangelo, who
may also have made preliminary
drawings for this major work.

that the body would already have started to rot, but Jesus insisted. Then he ordered
Lazarus to come out, and he did so, still wrapped in the burial cloths. Jesus told them to
unbind him so that he could go free.

The raising of Lazarus is the most dramatic example in the gospels of the divine
power Jesus had at his disposal, and also of his humanity. It is the culmination of the
seven miracles John selected as 'signs' pointing towards Jesus's own death and
resurrection.

The Resurrection of Lazarus
Giotto di Bondone (*c*1267–1337),
Scrovegni Chapel, Padua.

This fresco from the great series commissioned by Enrico Scrovegni in
1306 depicts Jesus confronting the newly-raised Lazarus in the doorway of
his tomb. Martha and Mary are prostrate at Jesus's feet and the onlookers
show amazement.

Lazarus Raised from the Dead
Michelangelo Buonarotti
(1475–1564), British Museum,
London.

One of the hundreds of unfinished Michelangelo sketches, Lazarus is
shown in the last stages of divesting himself of his grave-clothes just after
Jesus has raised him to life again.

THE TRIUMPHAL ENTRY INTO JERUSALEM

All this was done, that it might be fulfilled which was spoken by the prophet, saying, Tell ye the daughter of Sion, Behold, thy King cometh unto thee, meek, and sitting upon an ass, and a colt the foal of an ass.

Matt 21:4-5

The triumphal entry of Jesus into Jerusalem, at the end of the journey from the far north accompanied by his disciples, also marks the end of his attempts to keep his true identity secret from everyone but his closest associates. Jesus wished to be accepted only on his own terms and so he had spent more than two years shaping the understanding of his disciples. Now he threw caution to the winds and deliberately employed the traditional Hebrew symbolism associated with the Messiah.

The Jews expected the Messiah to appear on the Mount of Olives, the hill immediately to the east of Jerusalem separated from the city walls by the narrow valley of the River Kidron and looking across into the great Temple enclosure. It is still the place where Jews most wish to be buried. Jesus began his entry into the city from the Mount of Olives.

Well known prophecies about the Messiah in Isaiah and Zechariah speak of him entering his capital city humbly on a donkey, so Jesus had arranged for a donkey to be tethered ready for him on the Mount of Olives, and he sent two of the disciples to fetch it. They were given a message which would identify them if anyone questioned them.

126

And the multitudes that went before, and that followed, cried, saying, Hosanna to the Son of David; Blessed is he that cometh in the name of the Lord; Hosanna in the highest.

Matt. 21:9

The Entry into Jerusalem
Hans Acker, Besserer Chapel,
Ulm Cathedral, Germany.

This 15th-century stained-glass window depicts Jesus's carefully staged entry into Jerusalem at the end of his final journey. Spreading branches from trees and their garments on the road, his disciples and the crowd are acclaiming him as the Messiah.

The symbolism was derived from the entry of a Hebrew king after victory over the nation's enemies when he no longer had need of armour and war-horse.

Some of the disciples spread their cloaks on the donkey for Jesus to sit on; others spread their clothes on the road and cut branches from trees as further signs of a royal welcome, helped by the large crowd which had gathered for the event. When all the preparations for the procession had been completed, Jesus mounted the donkey, rode down the Mount of Olives, crossed the Kidron Valley and entered Jerusalem near the Temple.

Jerusalem was already beginning to fill with pilgrims for the most important of the three pilgrimage festivals of the Jewish year, the feast of Passover and Unleavened Bread, which was due to begin five days later and would last for eight days. Hebrew religious law required all Jews to go to Jerusalem for these festivals, and many arrived there from all over the ancient world.

The pilgrimage festivals had their own traditional ritual for the procession of the pilgrims to the Temple area when the pilgrims sang special psalms. Some of these psalms feature the Hebrew acclamation 'hallelujah', meaning 'Give praise to Yahweh', the Hebrew proper name of God. The words shouted by the crowd lining the route for Jesus were taken from Psalm 118, one of the hallelujah psalms:

'He is blessed who comes in Yahweh's name;

From Yahweh's house we bless you!'

They also shouted the acclamation 'hosanna', meaning 'we beseech you to save', to which they added the Messianic title 'Son of David'. Some acclaimed him King of Israel, and some shouted that this was the beginning of 'the coming kingdom of our father David'.

It was hardly surprising that Pharisees in the crowd called out for Jesus to rebuke his disciples and the crowd, and to stop them acclaiming him in such terms, but Jesus only replied that if the crowd was silent the very stones would acclaim him. The symbolism openly adopted by Jesus, and the acclamations he accepted, made the event an unmistakeable claim by Jesus to be the Messiah.

While he had such adulation from the crowd, the Jewish religious authorities could take no steps against Jesus without provoking an uncontrollable riot. Their opportunity would come towards the end of the week when the crowd found that Jesus was not fulfilling the kind of expectations they had of the Messiah.

Jesus completed his formal entry into the city by going to the Temple.

THE TRADERS IN THE TEMPLE

And he taught, saying unto them, Is it not written, My house
shall be called of all nations the house of prayer? but ye have
made it a den of thieves.

Mark 11:17

As Jesus entered the complex of courtyards in the sacred enclosure
surrounding the Temple itself, he would be moving into a market
place serving the needs of pilgrims and exploiting them. Some stalls
would be selling animals, especially doves and sheep, needed for the sacrifices all Jews
were required to offer at such occasions as the birth of a son. Some sold incense, which
was burned as a sacrifice in its own right, or which accompanied other sacrifices. Some
changed secular money into the only coinage acceptable to the Temple authorities for
payment of religious taxes.

Jesus would have seen all this on his previous visits to Jerusalem, and John's Gospel
records that he had reacted with violence on his first visit as an adult three years earlier.
Now he began to disrupt the market in earnest, overturning stalls and stopping people
using the Temple courtyards as a short-cut or for secular business. He was watched by
the crowd which had just acclaimed him as Messiah on his entry into the city.

As he laid about him, Jesus explained his actions with quotations from the prophets.
Most of the Temple area was strictly reserved for Jews and there were notices warning
Gentiles that they would be sentenced to death if they trespassed into it; Jesus shouted
out Isaiah's Messianic prophecy that the Temple would become a house of prayer for all
nations. Then he called on Jeremiah's fierce denunciation of the Temple authorities in
his day, that they had made God's house a den of thieves.

The Temple area was policed by Levites, but any move to arrest Jesus in the face of a
sympathetic crowd would have been futile. Moreover, the whole scene was overlooked by
the Jerusalem headquarters of the Roman garrison, and a serious riot would have
brought a detachment of Roman soldiers. But the Hebrew religious leaders began
seriously to plan the death of this Galilean who was now openly claiming that he was the
Messiah.

THE TEMPLE
CONTROVERSIES

And when he was come into the Temple, the chief priests and
the elders of the people came unto him as he was teaching, and
said, By what authority doest thou these things? and who gave
thee this authority?

Matt. 21:23

The Hebrew chief priests and other members of the Great Council
moved with all the caution of professional lawyers when they began
their moves against Jesus. They first approached him where he sat
teaching among the crowds in the Temple courtyards, as any Jew could do, and asked
him who gave him the authority to act so violently against authorized Temple traders.

Jesus replied by asking them where they thought John the Baptist had got his
authority to baptize. As John had been universally revered by the people they were
caught in a dilemma. If they admitted that he was inspired by God they could be asked
why they had ignored him; if they denied it they would provoke the resentment of the
people. They told Jesus that they did not know, and Jesus replied that he would not tell
them where he got his authority.

The exchange was only the start of continuous public argument between Jesus and
the religious authorities during the first four days of the time remaining to him. Jesus
himself attacked them with a parable which echoed a famous denunciation by the
prophet Isaiah.

A man planted a vineyard, said Jesus, let it out to tenants and went abroad. When it

began to bear, he sent agents for his rent but the tenants only assaulted them. Finally, he sent his son in the belief that they would treat him with more respect. But the tenants killed him, thinking that they would inherit the vineyard and be troubled no more. On the contrary, said Jesus, the owner would come himself, kill the tenants and give the vineyard to others.

The application would be clear to all, for Isaiah had said that the vineyard was the people of Israel, and to emphasize this Jesus quoted from the psalm the crowd had used to acclaim him as Messiah:

> The stone the builders rejected
>> has become the cornerstone;
> Yahweh has done this,
>> and it is wonderful to see.

Christ expels Idolators from the Temple
Giotto di Bondone (*c*1267–1337)
Scrovegni Chapel, Padua (right).

Another of the frescoes from the series begun in 1306, the lions and horses on the Temple hint at Venice, with which Padua had frequently been at war. The people Jesus drove out were traders, rather than idolators, serving the throngs of Jewish pilgrims.

THE WEDDING FEAST

And when the king came in to see the guests, he saw there a
man which had not on a wedding garment: and he saith unto
him, Friend, how camest thou in hither not having a wedding
garment? And he was speechless. Then said the king to the
servants, Bind him hand and foot, and take him away.

Matt. 22:11-13

Jesus told the parable of the Wedding Feast to the crowds of ordinary Jews
who had come to Jerusalem for the Passover festival, and it questioned
whether they had really responded to God's choice of them.

Jesus used his parables many times, and there is more than one version of this one. In
this version Jesus said that the kingdom of Heaven was like a king who gave a great
feast for the marriage of his son, but the people he asked all made excuses for refusing his
invitation. One said he had bought a field which he must see; for another it was a yoke
of oxen to try; a third had just got married himself. So the king revoked all the
invitations and sent his servants out to fill his wedding feast with the poor, the blind
and the injured, if necessary compelling them to come.

When the king went in to his crowded feast to greet his unusual guests he noticed
that one of them was not wearing one of the festive garments specially provided, so he
had him thrown out and punished. Jesus ended the parable by saying that many were
called but few were chosen.

With this story Jesus gave notice to the crowds who flocked to hear him that they

Mosaic depicting the head of
Christ, Museum of St. Mark's,
Venice.

There shall be weeping and gnashing of teeth.
For many are called, but few are chosen.

Matt 22:13-14

would be judged by the same standards as their leaders. If riches and power created problems, it did not follow that poverty and deprivation guaranteed entry into the kingdom of God.

His attention was drawn back to the official guardians of the nation's religion by their arrival to put a series of questions designed to trap him. One was about the morality of paying Roman taxes; Jesus countered by pointing to the emperor's image on the coins they used. If people knew when to use secular coins, he said, they knew how to balance their loyalty to the secular powers and their loyalty to God. Sadduccees, who did not believe in resurrection, put a question to him about marriage in the after-life, designed to make a fool of him. Jesus replied that they must revise their beliefs about heaven.

THE LAST
JUDGEMENT

Nation shall rise against nation, and kingdom against kingdom:
and great earthquakes shall be in divers places, and famines, and
pestilences; and fearful sights and great signs shall there be from
heaven.

Luke 21:10-11

*The Last Judgement and Resurrection
of the Dead*
From the Psalter of Ingeburg of
Denmark, Musée Condé,
Chantilly, France (right).

Invited by his disciples to admire
the Temple in Jerusalem, Jesus
warned them of the coming
judgement of all people, living or
dead, when the Temple would be
destroyed. This 13th-century
illuminated manuscript depicts
Jesus as the 'Son of Man' who will
come to earth on the clouds of
heaven to judge.

When the religious leaders had finished trying to argue with him Jesus launched into an extensive denunciation of the scribes and Pharisees again, but this time in their centre of power, the Temple area. Then he lamented over Jerusalem and its reputation for killing prophets: 'How often would I have gathered her children together, even as a hen gathereth her chickens under her wings, and ye would not!'

Some of his disciples wanted him to come and admire the magnificent Temple itself, whose rebuilding had begun 49 years earlier and would continue for a further 34 years after Jesus's death. But Jesus refused and said that the days were coming when no stone of it would be left standing on another.

He left the area and crossed the Kidron valley to the Mount of Olives where he could look across at the whole splendour of the Temple and the courtyards and colonnades which surrounded it. Peter, James, John and Andrew approached him there and asked when the destruction he had just foretold would happen, and if there would be any warning signs.

Jesus first warned them that there would be many false Messiahs, wars would break

out, and there would be famines and earthquakes, but this would only be the beginning of the birth-pangs. His disciples, he continued, would be denounced before kings and councils for preaching the gospel, but they must not worry how to answer the charges because the Holy Spirit would inspire them.

The chaos would develop, said Jesus, with members of families betraying and hating each other, false prophets leading people astray, a general increase in evil and many of his followers growing cold in their love. So far he had painted a picture of a dying civilization rather than a cosmic calamity, and he added an optimistic note: those who endured to the end would be saved, and his gospel of the Kingdom of God would be preached to the ends of the earth.

In the second part of his discourse Jesus spoke in a much darker vein. The final phase would begin, he said, with 'the desolating horror' standing in the holy place. This was originally a pagan altar erected in the Hebrew Temple by Greek conquerors for the Jews to worship; it desecrated the Temple, provoked a war, and became the symbol of ultimate blasphemy and of the Antichrist. When this appeared, warned Jesus, everyone should flee as if a ruthless invader had suddenly appeared. There would be a period of great suffering which no one could survive unless God shortened it for the sake of the ones he had chosen.

The devastation would extend to the universe itself, Jesus continued, with the sun and moon darkened and the stars falling. Then all the survivors would see 'the Son of Man' coming on the clouds of heaven with power and great glory. This apocalyptic figure and his title comes from the prophet Daniel, who said he would be sent by God at the end of time, as conqueror and judge with an angelic army. He would defeat and punish all God's enemies, and inaugurate the era of God's eternal rule.

At this stage, Jesus concluded, the Son of Man would send out angels with trumpets to gather together all those chosen by God for salvation 'from the four winds, from the uttermost part of the earth to the uttermost part of heaven'.

In this description of the final days Jesus drew heavily on popular Hebrew apocalyptic writings, such as the Book of Daniel, which would be familiar to his listeners. Originally these cryptic writings gave encouragement in times of persecution, in language which would be clear to the persecuted but obscure to their conquerors. There is no way of knowing whether Jesus meant his listeners to take him literally, or whether he too was using vivid symbolism to warn them to expect disaster and persecution.

The Temple area in Jerusalem was levelled by the Romans 40 years later at the end of a war against Jewish extremists.

Immediately after the tribulation of those days shall the sun be darkened, and the moon shall not give her light, and the stars shall fall from heaven, and the powers of the heavens shall be shaken.

Matt 24:29

The Last Judgement
Peter von Cornelius (1783–1867),
Ludwigskirche, Munich.

The influential German artist Cornelius tried to return to Renaissance principles of painting particularly in his murals, of which this is a fine example. Jesus in glory is seated on the clouds of heaven, presiding over the work of the angels of judgement as they separate the saved from the damned.

137

THE WISE AND
FOOLISH VIRGINS

If the goodman of the house had known in what watch the thief
would come, he would have watched, and would not have
suffered his house to be broken up. Therefore be ye also ready:
for in such an hour as ye think not the Son of Man cometh.

Matt. 24:43-44

The last reported teaching of Jesus to ordinary people before his arrest, trial and execution was all about personal responsibility and judgement. It gains an added emphasis from its position in the gospels. Jesus made his points with three parables.

In the parable of the Ten Virgins, Jesus drew on a familiar sight at weddings. The bridegroom was met by virgins carrying lamps who escorted him to his house for the wedding ceremony. In Jesus's story the bridegroom did not appear until midnight, by which time the virgins' lamps had all but gone out. Only five of them had a spare supply of oil, and they refused to help the rest in case they too had insufficient. Jesus told his listeners that they must watch, because they did not know when their Lord might come.

The parable of the Talents turns on capital a man entrusted to his servants to invest while he was away. The talent was a unit of weight - whether 20.5 or 41 kilogrammes is not certain - which in monetary terms usually referred to a weight of silver. One servant received five talents, another two, and a third only one; even 20.5 kilogrammes of silver would be a lot of money. All doubled their investment by the time their master returned except the servant entrusted with only one talent. He buried it because he was afraid of

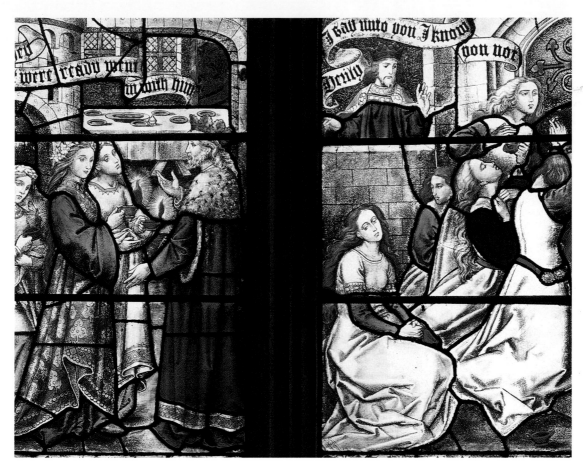

The Parable of the Wise and Foolish Virgins
Hillesden Church, Bucks.

These two adjacent 19th-century stained-glass windows depict the parable of judgement told by Jesus, in which half of the maidens engaged to accompany the bridegroom to the wedding feast run out of oil for their lamps because he is later than they expect. They are excluded from the feast.

losing it, and for his cowardliness had it given to the richest of his colleagues while he was thrown out.

Finally, in the parable of the Sheep and the Goats, a judge separated sheep from goats. The criteria for judging which were sheep, destined for blessedness, and which were goats, destined for damnation, were the deeds done to the deprived. Jesus identified himself with the deprived, and told his listeners that whatever they did, or did not do, for one of the most insignificant of the deprived, they did it – or not – to him; and by that they would be judged by God. In a strange way, it was as powerful a claim to be God's Son as any Jesus ever made.

139

JUDAS PLANS TO BETRAY JESUS

Then one of the twelve, called Judas Iscariot, went unto the chief priests, and said unto them, What will ye give me, and I will deliver him unto you? And they covenanted with him for 30 pieces of silver.

Matt. 26:14-15

J udas Iscariot's offer to betray Jesus marked the beginning of his 'Passion' during the Thursday and Friday of his last week in Jerusalem. It began with the Passover meal he ate with his disciples, and continued with his agony of anticipation in the Garden of Gethsemane, his arrest, examinations, legal trials and humiliations. It ended with his execution by crucifixion and his burial.

At an informal meeting in the high priest's house the religious leaders had already decided that Jesus must be killed. The problem Jesus posed for them was more political than religious; if his following continued to increase, there would be riots which the Romans would quell and they would remove what remained of Jewish autonomy. That year's high priest, Caiaphas, gave the meeting the justification for removing Jesus: it was better, he said, that one man should die for the people rather than the whole nation perish.

While Jesus still enjoyed the adulation of the crowd he could not be openly arrested, but there were signs that his popularity was waning as people found that he was not the kind of Messiah they expected. At that point Judas Iscariot went to the chief priests and

Judas Accepts the Bribe
Exeter Cathedral.

This stained-glass window depicts Judas with the Jewish chief priests accepting the 30 pieces of silver. In exchange Judas agreed to let them know where they could arrest Jesus without risk of a riot. In the event, Judas returned the money after the arrest and hanged himself.

offered to show them where they could arrest Jesus quietly without the danger of provoking a riot. As one of the twelve disciples he would know where Jesus planned to be. The chief priests agreed to pay Judas 30 pieces of silver, the equivalent of a month's pay for a labourer.

The gospels do not say why Judas decided to do it. He may have concluded that Jesus was not really the Messiah when he failed to begin the nationalist religious rising so many expected. Jesus had flaunted his Messianic claim when he entered Jerusalem four days earlier, but since then he had seemed to do nothing except irritate many different groups with his condemnations. If he was not the Messiah he had to be removed.

THE LAST SUPPER

> Jesus took bread, and blessed it, and brake it, and gave it to the
> disciples, and said, Take, eat; this is my body. And he took the
> cup, and gave thanks, and gave it to them, saying, Drink ye all of
> it; for this is my blood of the new testament, which is shed for
> many for the remission of sins.
>
> Matt. 26:26-28

The feast of Passover and Unleavened Bread began on a Friday that year, and as Jews started each new day at sunset, the Passover meal would be held after sunset on Thursday. The day before was 'Preparation Day'; the Passover lambs were killed at noon, followed by the preparation and cooking of the Passover meal to be eaten that evening as Passover began.

Jesus and his disciples had been staying each night at Bethany, and Jesus told Peter and John to go into Jerusalem, where they would find a man waiting to lead them to the place where Jesus had arranged for them to eat their Passover meal. When they reached the place they would discover an upper room furnished and ready with all that they needed for the celebration of the feast. They would recognize him, said Jesus, because – unusually for a man – he would be carrying a pitcher of water, and Jesus had also arranged a password. Jesus would have taken elaborate precautions to keep the venue secret because he realized that he was now at risk if the authorities knew where he would be.

The Passover originated as a nomadic shepherds' festival to invoke God's protection against evil forces, particularly when moving from one pasture to another. Its central feature was the sacrifice of a lamb whose blood, the life-force filled with God's power,

The Last Supper
The Master of the Reredos of the
Church of St. Francisco, Museu
Nacional de Arte Antiga, Lisbon.

The 16th-century reredos painted
for the main church of Evora in
Portugal depicts Jesus and his
disciples during their last meal
together before his arrest. The
disciples would have been
portrayed as recognizable local
dignitaries.

142

was smeared round the doorway of tents and houses to repel any evil. The lamb was then eaten as a communion meal provided by God. At the great escape from Egypt the festival took on added significance as the commemoration of God's power to save his chosen people from slavery and the power of the Egyptian gods.

Jesus and the twelve disciples assembled in the upper room at sunset when the day of Passover began. It would be the last time that Jesus had the chance to speak extensively with them, and there is no indication that his mother or anyone else associated with him was present.

Originally, the Passover meal had been eaten in haste with everyone dressed for travelling, 'your sandals on your feet and your staff in your hand', to commemorate the haste of the escape from Egypt. In the course of time, it followed the normal conventions of a leisurely festive meal, with the participants sitting or reclining round a table. It was essentially a family occasion, but recognized groups like Jesus and the disciples might celebrate it together, particularly if they were away from home.

The main dish was roast lamb and the herbs associated with the semi-desert pastures of the nomadic shepherds, accompanied by bread and wine. The bread had to be baked without rising agents, again to symbolize the haste of their ancestors' Passover meal; hence the description 'unleavened bread' and the name of the festival which immediately followed the day of Passover. As they began to eat, Jesus took a normal, round flat loaf, and said the traditional Hebrew blessing over it: 'Blessed art thou, O Lord our God, King of the universe, who bringest forth bread from the earth.' Then as he broke the bread into pieces and passed it to the disciples, he added to the traditional words: 'Take, eat: this is my body, which is broken for you: this do in remembrance of me.'

The meal continued, perhaps for two hours or more, until it was time for the traditional blessing over a large cup of wine before passing it round for everyone to drink. Unlike the brief blessing of bread, this final blessing was long and elaborate. It recounted the saving acts of God from the creation of the world down to the present day, and particularly the miracle of the first 'passover', the great escape from Egypt. But before he passed the cup to his disciples, Jesus added the words, 'This cup is the new testament in my blood: this do ye, as oft as ye drink it, in remembrance of me.'

Jesus and his disciples celebrated their Passover meal, the Last Supper, during the opening hours of the day of Passover, just after sunset. In the course of the evening he turned this celebration into a commemoration of his own Messianic powers to liberate, and linked it with his death by crucifixion later in the same Jewish day between noon and three o'clock. That apparent disaster would turn into a triumph over death and evil, and by designating the bread and wine his body and blood he indicated that his followers could share in his victory.

During the meal, Jesus took off his main garment, girded himself with a towel and prepared to wash the disciples' feet. They protested, for this was a menial task normally performed by servants when guests were welcomed. Jesus dismissed their protests and indicated that his action meant that he had welcomed them to share in his life and the

But I say unto you, I will not drink henceforth of this fruit of the vine, until that day when I drink it new with you in my Father's kingdom.

Matt. 26:29

Communion of the Apostles
Fra Angelico (c1400–1455),
Museo di San Marco
dell'Angelico, Florence.

The fresco depicts the Last Supper
as a 15th-century Christian
communion service, rather than
the Jewish Passover meal it
actually was. The quotation is
from St. John's Gospel: 'Whoso
eateth my flesh, and drinketh my
blood, hath eternal life.'

glory he was about to earn. They should follow his example, he added, and do the same for each other; as his messengers they must also be servants.

Jesus then told the disciples that one of them would betray him, and each one anxiously asked him if he thought he was the one. Peter protested that he would go to prison or death with him, and Jesus replied that by daybreak Peter would three times have denied that he knew him. Perhaps to reassure him after saying that, Jesus quietly told Peter it would be the the one he next favoured with an affectionate morsel of food, then he dipped a little bread in wine, gave it to Judas Iscariot and told him to do what he had to do quickly. Judas left the meal to go about his betrayal of Jesus, but the other disciples thought that as the group's treasurer he had been sent to buy something.

After Jesus had ended the meal with the long ritual blessing of the final cup of wine, they all sang a psalm. Then they went out into the night, crossed the Kidron valley and made for the Garden of Gethsemane at the foot of the Mount of Olives. It was the nearest place to find quiet and solitude.

145

THE GARDEN OF GETHSEMANE

Then cometh Jesus with them unto a place called Gethsemane, and saith unto the disciples, Sit ye here, while I go and pray yonder.

Matt. 26:36

Jesus and the disciples had often been to the Garden of Gethsemane since their arrival in Jerusalem, so the other disciples would expect Judas to know where they had gone when he found they had all left the upper room. Only Jesus and Peter knew that he would probably be arriving with troops sent by the Sanhedrin.

Meanwhile, Jesus told most of the disciples to rest. He himself took the inner group of disciples, Peter, James and John, and went a little further into the garden. There he openly admitted to the three that he was consumed with anxiety to the point of death and asked them to stay awake with him. Then he moved forward and fell on his face in prayer.

Now that events were moving out of his control, Jesus's prayer expressed his profound fear of what was about to happen, and he prayed that if it were still possible he should be spared it: 'O my Father, if it be possible, let this cup pass from me: nevertheless not as I will, but as thou wilt.' Luke says that an angel came to stengthen him, and in the course of his prayer Jesus sweated blood.

When he turned back to the three disciples he found them asleep, so he wakened them and asked them why they could not watch even for an hour. He told them to watch

146

The Agony in the Garden
Francisco de Goya (1746–1828),
Christie's, London (right).

This painting of Jesus's agony of
anticipation in Gethsemane is
similar in composition to Goya's
1808 painting *The Third of May*
showing French troops executing
Spanish insurgents.

and pray, so that they would not be overwhelmed by what was about to happen, and
added that however willing they might be in spirit, the flesh was weak.

Jesus returned to his own vehement prayers, still asking the Father if the ordeal could
be avoided but that he would conform to his will. Again he found the three asleep, and
they were abashed when he woke them. He returned to his agonized prayers, and when
he found the three asleep for the third time he told them to sleep on. He had heard the
sound of the guard and told the three that the hour had come.

The sudden change of scene in the Garden of Gethsemane is conveyed dramatically
by the gospels. At one moment all was silence with Jesus praying near the sleeping
figures of the disciples, and the darkness only relieved by the full moon of the Passover

And while he yet
spake, lo, Judas,
one of the twelve,
came, and with
him a great
multitude with
swords and staves,
from the chief
priests and elders
of the people.

Matt 26:47

The Agony in the Garden
Andrea Mantegna (c1431–1506),
National Gallery, London.

As Jesus prays to be spared the
coming ordeal, angels show him
the instruments to be used in his
execution: the pillar of scourging,
the cross itself, and the spear. In
the background, the soldiers, led
by Judas, approach from a very
Italianate Jerusalem.

season. The next moment tumult broke out as Judas arrived with members of the Sanhedrin and soldiers from the Temple guard armed with swords and staves, all carrying torches and lanterns.

It might not have been clear to the guard which one was Jesus, so Judas had arranged to go up to him, greet him as Master and kiss him. Jesus countered this by addressing Judas as friend, then he asked him curtly if he was betraying the Son of Man with a kiss and told him to get on with what he had come to do.

The disciples began to fight the soldiers to stop them arresting Jesus, and Peter wounded one of the high priest's officials. Jesus shouted at them to stop and told them that those who take up the sword also die by it. Did they not think, he asked, that he could summon an army of angels if he wished? Jesus then healed the wounded man and, turning to the officials leading the party, he asked them why they had found it necessary to come at such a time and with such a show of force; they could have arrested him, he said, any time when he openly sat teaching in synagogues or in the Temple courtyards. 'But this is your hour,' Jesus added, 'and the power of darkness.'

At that point all the disciples fled from the scene as Jesus was arrested. A young man who had come to see what happened was also seized by the soldiers, but he managed to slip out of the loose linen cloak he was wearing and he fled naked into the night.

And forthwith he came to Jesus, and said, Hail, master; and kissed him.
And Jesus said unto him, Friend, wherefore art thou come?
Then came they, and laid hands on Jesus, and took him.

Matt. 26: 49-50

The Agony in the Garden
Sandro Botticelli (1445–1510),
Royal Chapel, Granada.

After the Last Supper, Jesus and his disciples went to the Garden of Gethsemane, where Jesus prayed in distress while he awaited his arrest. Botticelli depicts Jesus being strengthened by an angel, while the sleeping disciples and the sharply-pointed fence emphasize his loneliness and agony.

The Betrayal
Church of the Archangel Michael,
Pedoulas, Cyprus.

The 15th-century mural depicts the moment in the Garden of
Gethsemane when Judas addressed Jesus as 'Master', and kissed him to
show the high priest's soldiers which man they should arrest.

THE HIGH PRIEST'S EXAMINATION AND PETER'S DENIALS

And the Lord turned, and looked upon Peter. And Peter remembered the word of the Lord, how he had said unto him, Before the cock crow, thou shalt deny me thrice. And Peter went out, and wept bitterly.

Luke 22:61-62

After they had arrested Jesus in the Garden of Gethsemane, the armed party sent by the Sanhedrin bound him and took him to the high priest's house. The high priest was president of the Sanhedrin, the Jewish Great Council, and also the head of the priesthood, the hereditary priests who alone had the right to officiate at sacrifices. The Jewish king – himself a Roman puppet – appointed and deposed the high priests, who constituted an exclusive and elitist religious aristocracy.

Jesus was first taken to Annas, father-in-law of the current high priest, Caiaphas, for a preliminary examination before he was brought before Caiaphas and the full Sanhedrin. The actual trial of Jesus would have to wait for daybreak because trials were forbidden during the hours of darkness by the Sanhedrin's regulations but the court's leading members needed to frame the charges against Jesus and find out what defence he might make.

There were further problems too. There were less than 24 hours to the next sunset and the start of a sabbath, when the Sanhedrin could not sit. Moreover, the Romans severely limited the Sanhedrin's powers to inflict punishment; if Jesus was to be executed he would have to be taken before the Roman Procurator's court for trial and sentence under Roman law. And if he was then sentenced to death he would have to be executed before sunset because of the sabbath.

The high priest's house was thronged and the examination of Jesus was open to all. When the arresting party arrived with Jesus, Peter and an unnamed disciple were following to see what happened. As they took Jesus into the house the other disciple went right in behind him, but Peter stayed in the open doorway among a crowd of servants and guards warming themselves at a charcoal brazier. A servant girl asked him if he wasn't another of 'that man's' disciples. Peter denied it, and they all turned again to watch Annas begin questioning Jesus.

Annas first asked Jesus who his disciples were and what he had taught. If this dangerous movement was to be stamped out, it might be necessary to arrest the closest associates of Jesus as well. But Jesus refused to answer the question directly. In words similar to the ones he had used to the soldiers sent to arrest him, Jesus told Annas that he had taught openly in synagogues and in the Temple for all the world to hear. 'Why ask me?', Jesus continued, Annas could ask anyone who had heard him teach; they would know what he had said.

It was a clever reply because it diverted attention away from the disciples and directed Annas towards the crowds of people who had gathered to hear Jesus teach, both in Galilee and in Jerusalem. But it was also an impertinent tone for a prisoner. One of the guards struck Jesus across the face and told him that it was no way to address a high priest. Jesus asked the guard to explain to him the offence in what he had said, and if there was none could he explain why he had struck him.

Meanwhile, the people near Peter in the doorway were growing more convinced that he was a disciple of Jesus's, despite his denial to the servant girl. Another of the servants began to say to everyone that Peter was a companion of Jesus the Nazarene, this time mentioning the Galilean origins of them both. Peter hotly denied it with an oath.

Finally, a relative of the man Peter had wounded in the Garden of Gethsemane turned on Peter and said he had seen him when Jesus was arrested, and another pointed out that he spoke with a Galilean accent. Peter cursed and shouted again that he did not know Jesus. Jesus looked across the room towards Peter and the commotion around him, a cock crew as dawn approached and Peter went out to weep bitterly.

And they led Jesus away to the high priest: and with him were assembled all the chief priests and the elders and the scribes. And Peter followed him afar off.

Mark 14:53-54

154

Christ before the High Priest
Gerrit van Honthorst
(1590–1656), National Gallery,
London.

Immediately after his arrest, Jesus was taken to the high priest's house
where he was questioned about his teaching to prepare the charges for the
formal trial next day. At this stage Jesus refused to be drawn into
incriminating himself.

THE JEWISH AND
ROMAN TRIALS

As soon as it was day, the elders of the people and the chief
priests and the scribes came together, and led him into their
council, saying, Art thou the Christ?

Luke 22:66-67

The high priest Annas realized that he was getting nowhere with his
questioning of Jesus, so he gave up and left him under guard to await
the formal meeting of the Sanhedrin. With daybreak the Sanhedrin
convened, presided over by the ruling high priest, Caiaphas, and Jesus was brought
before it. Witnesses testified that Jesus had said he was able to destroy the Temple and
build it again in three days, words similar to earlier statements made by Jesus, but the
witnesses contradicted each other.

Caiaphas asked Jesus if he had anything to say about the witnesses' allegations, but
Jesus realized that their confused evidence would not be accepted by the court, so he said
nothing. Caiaphas then asked Jesus directly if he was the Christ, the Messiah, 'the Son of
the Blessed'. Jesus replied, 'I am.' That admission was enough to condemn him, but
Jesus removed any doubts when he then quoted the strongest of all the Messianic
prophecies. He told the court that they would see him as Son of Man, Daniel's title for
the Messiah, sitting at the right hand of power and coming to earth on the clouds of
heaven.

In the face of such an answer the court had no need of unreliable witnesses. Caiaphas
pronounced that Jesus's answer was blasphemy and asked the Sanhedrin for a verdict.

156

Christ before Herod
Yarnton Church, Oxfordshire.

Because he came from Galilee, Jesus was also examined by Herod Antipas, the Jewish ruler of Galilee, who was in Jerusalem for the Passover. Herod hoped Jesus would perform a miracle for him. This 15th-century stained-glass panel depicts Herod questioning Jesus, who refuses to reply.

157

The court condemned Jesus to death. As the Romans did not allow the Sanhedrin to carry out such a sentence, the verdict meant that Jesus would have to be brought before the Roman court.

Jesus received some rough handling while the Sanhedrin arranged for a hearing by the Roman Procurator, Pontius Pilate. Now that he had been condemned, his guards amused themselves by blindfolding and beating him, then asking him as the Messiah to tell them who had struck him.

When Judas found that the Sanhedrin had condemned Jesus to death he returned the 30 pieces of silver to the chief priests and hanged himself.

Shortly after the Sanhedrin had delivered its verdict Pontius Pilate convened his own, Roman court and the Jewish authorities brought Jesus before him. They charged him with perverting the nation, discouraging people from paying the tribute tax, claiming that he was the Messiah and calling himself king.

Pilate only asked Jesus about being a king, to which Jesus gave an ambiguous reply, and Pilate then told the chief priests that he could find no fault in him. They protested that Jesus had stirred up the people from Galilee to Judaea, and when Pilate realized that Jesus was a Galilean he sent him to Herod Antipas, the Jewish ruler of the Galilee area, who was in Jerusalem for the festival. Herod listened to denunciations of Jesus from members of the Sanhedrin, mocked him for a while and then sent him back to Pilate.

Pilate told the Jewish leaders that neither he nor Herod could find any fault in Jesus and that he intended to release him. At this, the Sanhedrin members concentrated on the kingship charge, as this was clearly the only one which Pilate might take seriously. They warned Pilate that if he did not listen to them they would denounce him to the Roman emperor for refusing to take a treason charge seriously. To test popular feelings, Pilate then had Jesus brought out onto the raised pavement before his official residence and said, 'Behold your king!', but the crowd only shouted for him to be crucified.

Finally, Pilate offered to release Jesus as the customary amnesty for the festival, but the crowd called for Barabbas, a condemned bandit. At that, Pilate called for water and washed his hands before them all to show that he considered himself innocent of any bloodshed, and condemned Jesus to crucifixion.

And straightway in the morning the chief priests held a consultation with the elders and scribes and the whole council, and bound Jesus, and carried him away, and delivered him to Pilate.

Mark 15:1

Ecce Homo (Behold the Man)
Joos van Craesbeeck
(*c*1605–1662), Johnny van
Haeften Gallery, London.

The Jewish high court condemned Jesus, but it had to send him for trial by the Roman Procurator, Pontius Pilate, because he alone could order an execution. Pilate found Jesus innocent, but the crowds called for crucifixion when Pilate displayed Jesus to them.

THE CRUCIFIXION

When they were come to the place, which is called Calvary,
there they crucified him, and the malefactors, one on the right
hand, and the other on the left.

Luke 23:33

By the time Pilate had given his final verdict it was mid-morning on the
Friday and Jesus and the other condemned men must be dead by sunset
or the sabbath would be defiled. The Roman soldiers immediately
started the lengthy process of execution by crucifixion with a scourging to weaken the
victims, then they put a crown of thorns and a purple robe on Jesus in mockery and
hailed him as King of the Jews.

The condemned men were made to carry the cross-bar of their crosses to a place called
Golgotha, meaning 'skull', outside the walls of Jerusalem, where they were to be
crucified. Evidently, Jesus could not manage the weight of his cross-bar, for an onlooker
named Simon, from Cyrene, was made to carry it for him. There were many women
lamenting as he went, but Jesus told them to weep for themselves and for their children
because of what was coming to the city. Other incidents traditionally associated with the
tragic procession to Golgotha are not in the gospels.

Jerusalem was twice destroyed, levelled and rebuilt within the next two centuries, so
it is no longer possible to be sure of the route the condemned men took, nor where
Golgotha was, but the Church of the Holy Sepulchre has been the traditional site since
at least the 4th century.

Christ Mocked and Crowned with Thorns
Hieronymus Bosch (c1450–1516),
National Gallery, London.

After being condemned to crucifixion, Jesus was given a crown of thorns by the Roman soldiers and mocked as a king. Bosch has depicted the incident as a satire of evil and sadistic human nature.

Normally in a Roman crucifixion, the uprights were already in position, the cross-bars were laid on the ground and the condemned were stripped and nailed or tied by their hands or wrists to them. The cross-bars were then lifted and fastened to the upright, and the victim's feet were nailed or tied to the upright just clear of the ground. Sometimes there was a support for the victim to sit astride. Death could take several days, but it could be hurried along by breaking the legs of the crucified.

The crucifixions took place about noon, and the customary notices were nailed on the crosses to say why the men had been condemned. Pilate ordered a notice above Jesus in Hebrew, Latin and Greek saying 'Jesus of Nazareth, King of the Jews'. The Jewish authorities asked for this to be changed to 'He said, I am King of the Jews', but Pilate said, 'What I have written, I have written.' The executioners were entitled to their victims' clothes and they cast lots for Jesus's seamless robe to avoid tearing it.

Jesus had refused the drugged wine offered to the condemned as an anodyne, and his first words after being crucified were, 'Father forgive them; for they know not what they do.' The spectators called on him to come down from the cross if he thought he was so powerful that he could rebuild the Temple in three days. Clearly, that phrase had become popular with the crowd.

One of the crucified thieves also called on Jesus to save them all, but the other one reminded him that they were justly condemned while Jesus was innocent. He asked Jesus to remember him when he came into his kingdom, and Jesus replied that he would indeed be with him that day in paradise.

Among the people watching were Jesus's mother and other women associated with him, and at least one of the disciples. Jesus told his mother that she should look on that disciple as her son, and he told the disciple to treat her as mother. The disciple took her into his own home.

At about three o'clock in the afternoon, Jesus shouted the first phrase of Psalm 22: 'My God, my God, why hast thou forsaken me?', which in his native Aramaic would begin *'Elahi, Elahi'*. Some of the crowd thought he was calling out for Elijah, who in popular tradition would accompany the Messiah when he came, and they watched closely to see if Elijah would come to rescue Jesus. He also cried out that he was thirsty, and someone soaked a sponge in the soldiers' vinegary wine and held it up on a stick for him to drink.

Jesus Scourged and Martyred by Jews Giotto di Bondone (c1267–1337), Scrovegni Chapel, Padua. (bottom right).

One of the great series of frescoes commissioned in 1306, it conflates a number of incidents recorded in the gospels when Jesus was mocked, struck and taunted between his arrest and crucifixion. The execution itself was carried out by Romans.

The Flagellation of Christ
Piero della Francesca
(*c*1420–1492), Galleria Nazionale
della Marche, Urbino.

Painted for the cathedral of
Urbino, the picture depicts the
scourging of Jesus while Pilate
watches. Set in 15th-century Italy,
the indifference of the three
courtiers is a scathing comment
on his noble contemporaries by
the artist.

*Landscape with Jerusalem,
Christ carrying the Cross and
Preparations on the hill of Calvary*
Lucas van Valkenborch
(*c*1530–1597), Christie's, London.

This magnificent imaginary landscape depicts Jerusalem as a walled
Christian city with the Temple set in its midst like a cathedral. The
procession to the crucifixion is just leaving Jerusalem and workmen and
soldiers prepare the execution site in the foreground.

Then were there
two thieves
crucified with him,
one on the right
hand, and another
on the left. And
they that passed by
reviled him,
wagging their
heads, and saying,
Thou that
destroyest the
temple, and
buildest it in three
days, save thyself.

Matt. 27:38-40

Green Christ (Breton Calvery)
Paul Gauguin (1848–1903)
Musée Royaux des Beaux-Arts de
Belgique, Brussels.

Although best known for his
Tahiti paintings, Gauguin loved
Brittany, where he painted
between 1886 and 1891. The
wildness and primitiveness he said
he found there is reflected in this
painting of Jesus after he had been
taken down from the cross.
Painted in 1889, it is set in
Brittany.

And one ran and filled a spunge full of vinegar, and put it on a reed, and gave him to drink, saying, Let alone; let us see whether Elias will come to take him down. And Jesus cried with a loud voice, and gave up the ghost.

Mark 15:36-37

The Crucifixion
El Greco (1541–1614), Prado, Madrid.

Trained in the Venetian school, Domenicos Theotocopoulos (nicknamed 'El Greco', 'the Greek') settled in Spain in 1576, where he expressed the intense spirituality of the Spain of his times in his paintings. Even in death and grief, Jesus and those present are transformed by ecstasy.

The Crucifixion
Mathias Grunewald
(*c*1470–1528), Unterlinden
Museum, Colmar.

When closed, the four-winged
altarpiece painted between 1510
and 1515 for the monastic church
at Eisenheim displays the
crucifixion. Jesus's hands indicate
that in his agony he is praying,
while John the Baptist and the
sacrificial symbol of the lamb and
cross emphasize Jesus as Saviour.

Jesus shouted out again with part of a psalm, this time 31:5, to say that he
committed his spirit to the Father. Then he said, 'It is finished,' and died. Observing the
way he died, the Roman centurion in charge of the execution said that he was indeed the
Son of God, or that he was a righteous man.

One of the gospels reports that there were dramatic incidents when Jesus died: the
Temple curtain, which hid the innermost sanctuary from the rest, split from top to
bottom; there was an earthquake; tombs opened and many people saw the dead walking
about Jerusalem.

By this time the religious leaders were becoming worried that the three condemned
men would still be alive and on their crosses at sunset when the sabbath began, so they
asked Pilate to hurry their deaths by ordering their legs to be broken. This was done to
the two thieves, but Jesus was found to be dead already, so a soldier just pushed a spear
into his side to make sure.

The crowd watching it all included many who had been sympathetic towards Jesus,
so it dispersed with mixed feelings, some of them beating their breasts. Watching from a
distance were a group composed of his disciples and women closely associated with him,
including Mary Magdalene.

The Crucifixion
Graham Sutherland (1903–1980),
St. Matthew's Church,
Northampton.

Most famed for his great tapestry of Christ triumphant for the post-war
Coventry Cathedral, Sutherland was deeply influenced by his experiences
as an Official War Artist during the Second World War. His *Crucifixion*,
commissioned in the 1840s, is an uncompromising presentation of
dereliction.

THE BURIAL OF JESUS

This man went unto Pilate, and begged the body of Jesus. And he took it down, and wrapped it in linen, and laid it in a sepulchre that was hewn in stone, wherein never man before was laid.

Luke 23:52-53

Late on the Friday afternoon, after Jesus had died, two members of the Sanhedrin, the Great Council of Jews, came forward as friends who wished to make proper and reverent provision for his body. Neither of them had taken part in the Sanhedrin trial of Jesus. With the sabbath due to start as soon as the sun set, when nothing could be done for 24 hours, it was important to get Jesus's body buried quickly.

One of them, Joseph of Arimathea, was sufficiently important to be able to go straight to Pilate and obtain his permission to take the body down from the cross and bury it. The other, the Nicodemus who had gone to Jesus secretly by night during an earlier Passover, arrived to help with some 50 kilogrammes of burial spices.

The two men took the body off the cross and carried it to a nearby garden where Joseph of Arimathea owned a tomb. Carved out of the rock, the tomb was sealed by rolling a stone across its entrance. There they wrapped the body in linen cloths with the spices, rolled the stone across and left. It was a hurried affair, but some of the women planned to return to the tomb as soon as the sabbath was ended to make sure everything had been done properly.

Next morning, sabbath or not, a delegation from the Sanhedrin waited on Pilate and asked him to put a guard on the tomb. They quoted one of the claims Jesus had made, that he would rise again from death after three days, and said they were afraid that some of his disciples might steal the body and say that Jesus had fulfilled his prediction. That, they said, would only make the situation worse than it was before. Pilate told them to go and use their own guards, so they went to the tomb, sealed it and left it guarded.

170

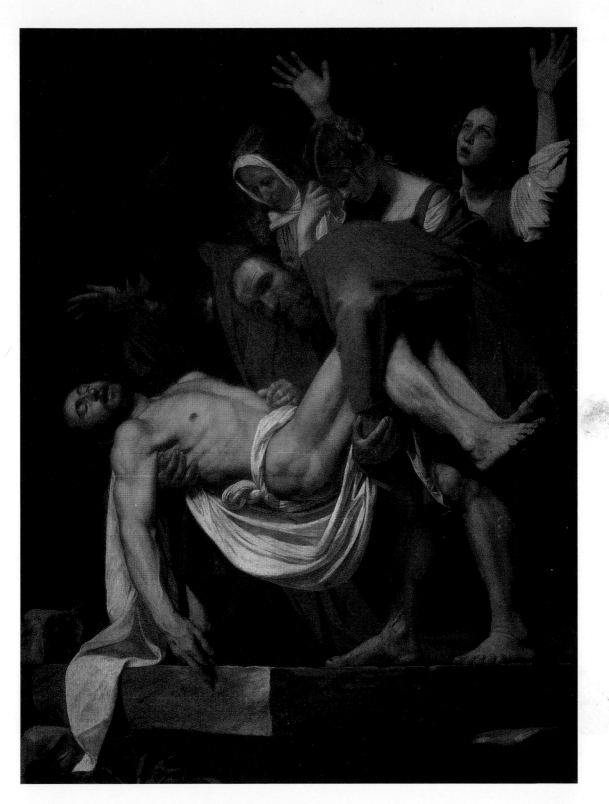

171

THE EMPTY TOMB

And very early in the morning the first day of the week, they
came unto the sepulchre at the rising of the sun. And they said
among themselves, Who shall roll us away the stone from the
door of the sepulchre? And when they looked, they saw that the
stone was rolled away.

Mark 16:2-4

Saturday sabbath, the last day of the Jewish week when work was forbidden,
ended at sunset, but the three women waiting to tend to the body of Jesus
did not start out until sunrise when there would be enough daylight to
work in the tomb. They wondered among themselves who would roll away the heavy
stone for them, which had been left sealing the entrance at sunset on Friday, but as they
approached the tomb they saw that the stone had already been moved.

The gospels give varying accounts of what happened next. One of the women, Mary
Magdalene, ran straight off to tell Peter and John that the body had gone and no one
knew where it had been taken. The others went into the tomb and saw at least one figure
in dazzlingly white clothes, who told them not to be afraid or amazed. The figure
explained that Jesus was not there because he had risen from the dead as he said he
would. The women were invited to see the place where Jesus had been laid, and then
they were told to go and tell his disciples.

Their first reaction was to flee from the tomb in terror, and to say nothing to anyone
because they were so afraid. Meanwhile, Mary Magdalene had told Peter and John, who

The Deposition and the Rolling Away of the Stone
Stanley Spencer (1891–1959),
York City Art Gallery.

In this work painted in 1956, Spencer depicts a Jesus unmarked by his ordeal with only the pallor of his skin suggesting death. Mary is a modern housewife fainting with grief. The panel below shows an angel opening the tomb ready for the resurrection of Jesus while the guards sleep.

Jesus saith unto her, Mary. She turned herself, and saith unto him, Rabboni; which is to say, Master. Jesus saith unto her, Touch me not.

John 20:16-17

Noli me Tangere (Do not Touch Me)
Fra Angelico (*c*1400–1455),
Museo di San Marco
dell'Angelico, Florence.

One of the frescoes in the monks' cells of San Marco painted about 1441, this one depicts the moment when Jesus, newly risen from the dead, reveals himself to Mary Magdalene by calling her name.

immediately ran to the tomb. John got there first and saw the linen grave cloths from the doorway but did not go in. Peter arrived, went straight in and noticed that the cloth used to wrap the body's head was separate from the other cloths and still rolled up. He called John in, and the position of the cloths convinced them both that Jesus had risen as he said he would. They then left the empty tomb and went back to the place where they had been staying.

Sometime in the previous 24 hours the guards had left the tomb. They told the chief priests that there had been an earth tremor, and an angel had appeared and rolled back the stone from the entrance to the tomb; they added that they had been too terrified to do anything. Caiaphas hurriedly convened a meeting of the Sanhedrin, and they decided to bribe the guards to say that Jesus's disciples had stolen the body while the guards slept. The councillors promised the guards that if Pilate heard about it they would see that they came to no harm.

By the time Mary Magdalene returned to the tomb Peter and John had left, so she did not know that they thought Jesus had risen from the dead. Weeping outside the opening, she looked in to the tomb and saw two figures sitting where the body had been. They asked her why she wept. She told them that her Lord had been taken and she did not know where they had put him, then she turned away again.

Half facing her in the garden was Jesus, but she did not recognize him and thought he was a gardener. She asked him to tell her where he had put the body if he had taken it away. Jesus just addressed her by her name, Mary. She turned fully to him and said 'Rabboni!', a more solemn form of address than 'Rabbi'. Jesus told her not to touch him, or to stop touching him, because he had not yet ascended to his Father. Then he asked her to go to the disciples and tell them that he was ascending to his Father and theirs, to his God and theirs.

Mary went to the place where some of the disciples had by now gathered, possibly the upper room of the Last Supper, told them that she had seen Jesus and delivered her message. She was the first person to see Jesus after his resurrection.

174

EMMAEUS

Supper at Emmaus
Rembrandt van Rijn (1606–69), Louvre, Paris.

In this 1648 painting, Rembrandt depicts the moment when the two disciples realize that it was Jesus, risen from the dead, who had just walked with them from Jerusalem. They had told him about the terrible events culminating in the crucifixion, and Jesus had explained why this had to happen to the Messiah.

Later on the Sunday, two of Jesus's followers were walking to their home in Emmaeus, some two miles east of Jerusalem. On the way they were joined by a man they took to be a stranger, who entered into conversation with them and asked them what had been happening.

They told him about the events of the previous week, that 'Jesus of Nazareth, a prophet mighty in deed and word before God and all the people' had been condemned to death by the Sanhedrin and crucified. They had hoped, they said, that he would be the redeemer of Israel, and it had all happened three days ago.

Some of the women in their group, they continued, had been to his tomb, but they reported that Jesus's body had gone and that angels had told them he was alive. Others had gone to the tomb and confirmed the women's account, they said, but they had not seen Jesus. Then Jesus, whom they still did not recognize, reminded them of the passages in the Hebrew scriptures which predicted that the Messiah would suffer like that before entering into his glory.

By now they had reached Emmaeus and Jesus began to walk on, but the two men persuaded him to come to their home for the night as it was almost dusk. There the three of them sat down to a meal, during which Jesus took bread, blessed it, broke it in pieces and gave it to them.

It was a normal feature of any meal, but there must have been something characteristic about the way Jesus did it, for the two suddenly realized who their guest was, at which Jesus disappeared. They said to each other that this accounted for the way he had enthralled them as he expounded the prophecies to them, and they went straight back to Jerusalem to tell the disciples.

JERUSALEM
& GALILEE

Behold my hands and my feet, that it is I myself; handle me and see; for a spirit hath not flesh and bones, as ye see me have.

Luke 24:39

Most of the disciples had gathered together by sunset on the Sunday, and had locked themselves in because they were afraid of what the Jewish authorities might do next. As they were listening to the two men from Emmaeus, Jesus appeared among them.

They were terrified, and Jesus tried to calm them down. He showed them his hands and feet with the wounds from the crucifixion nails, to reassure them that he was flesh and blood rather than a ghost, but understandably they were not convinced. So Jesus asked them to give him some of the fish they were about to eat, and he ate it in front of them.

Jesus explained how the Messianic prophecies in the Hebrew scriptures referred to him, as he had done for the two men on the way to Emmaeus. He went on to tell them that all authority had been given him in heaven and on earth, and that they were to go out into all the world, and baptize believers in the name of the Father, the Son and the Holy Spirit. Jesus then breathed on them and told them that they had received the Holy Spirit, and that they could forgive or retain anyone's sins.

Thomas, one of the disciples, was not present on this first Sunday evening after the crucifixion, and when the other disciples told him about it he said that he would not believe any of it unless he could see Jesus, and feel the wounds made by crucifying. The next Sunday Jesus appeared again to the disciples with Thomas there. Jesus invited

Thomas to touch his wounds, he was convinced that it really was Jesus, and he addressed him as 'my Lord and my God'.

Jesus had begun his mission in Galilee nearly three years earlier, and the angels in the empty tomb said that he was going to Galilee and wished the disciples to be there. Seven of them, whose trade was fishing, returned to their boats on the sea of Galilee.

They fished all one night without success, and by the light of the dawn saw a man standing on the shore without realising that it was Jesus. He called out to ask if they had caught anything, and when they replied that they had been unsuccessful he told them to cast their nets on the starboard side of the boat. They did so, and caught so many that the net was too heavy to haul aboard.

John realized who it was and said to Peter, 'It is the Lord!' The boat was about 100 yards out, so Peter, who was naked, tied a garment around himself and jumped overboard to wade ashore. The others made for the shore in the boat, towing the net. They found that Jesus had brought bread with him and was cooking fish on a fire he had lit. He told Peter to fetch some of the fish they had caught and invited them all to eat.

After they had eaten, Jesus three times asked Peter if he loved him, and Peter replied with increasing vehemence that he did. After each affirmation Jesus told him to feed his sheep or look after his lambs. He then warned him that when he was young he had girded himself and walked where he wished, but when he grew old he would be bound and taken where he did not want to go; then Jesus told him to follow him. Peter interpreted this as referring to the way he would die.

Pointing to John, Peter asked what would happen to him, and Jesus asked what concern it was of Peter's if he wanted John to stay behind until he came. His reply started a rumour that John would not die.

Simon Peter went up, and drew the net to land full of great fishes, an hundred and fifty and three: and for all there were so many, yet was not the net broken. Jesus saith unto them, Come and dine. And none of the disciples durst ask him, Who art thou? knowing that it was the Lord.

John 21:11-12

THE ASCENSION

The risen Jesus appeared and disappeared again on a number of occasions after his first appearance on the Sunday following his execution, but his ascension was in a different category. It indicated that this would be the last of his earthly appearances to the group he had called and chosen at the beginning of his mission.

The gospels locate the incident on the eastern side of Jerusalem, where the road to Bethany climbs over the Mount of Olives. It was on the traditional Messianic route which Jesus had chosen for his solemn entry into Jerusalem at the beginning of his last days of mortal life, and the manner of his leaving had the same Messianic associations. According to the Acts of the Apostles, a continuation of Luke's Gospel, the disciples had asked Jesus if the time had come for him to restore the kingdom to Israel, which the Messiah was expected to bring about when he came.

Jesus replied that they were not to be told the timetable decided by the Father, but they would receive the full power of the Holy Spirit, another of the events expected of the Messianic era. Then, continued Jesus, they would be his witnesses not only in Jerusalem but throughout Judaea and Samaria and to the most remote parts of the earth. With that, he was lifted upwards and a cloud hid him from their sight.

The disciples returned from the Mount of Olives to their lodgings in Jerusalem, the upper room which had been the scene of the Last Supper. With them were some of the women who had been followers of Jesus, his mother and other close relatives.

Jesus had told them that he would always be with them, and that he was going to prepare a place for them. His ascension marked the end of his visible leadership of the group and the beginning of the disciples' responsibilities as apostles and as leaders of a church.

And it came to pass, while he blessed them, he was parted from them, and carried up into heaven.

Luke 24:51

The Ascension
Ford Madox Brown (1821–1893), Forbes Magazine Collection, New York.

Reminiscent of a baroque church ceiling, Brown's painting depicts the moment when Jesus ascended to heaven to assume his role as Lord of the universe. The angels are telling the disciples that Jesus will come again.

CHRONOLOGY OF JESUS AND THE NEW TESTAMENT

The four gospels were not written down in the form familiar to us in the New Testament until at least 30 years after the death of Jesus Christ. During those years the source material existed in writings now lost to us or in oral traditions. The broad outline of the chronology of the New Testament given below would be accepted by most conservative Christians, even if they question some of the detail. It is worth noticing that most of Paul's letters were written before the first of the gospels. An ancient Christian historian referred to an earlier form of Matthew's Gospel written in Aramaic (the language spoken by Jesus) but we do not know what it contained.

It seems strange to date the birth of Jesus Christ at 6BC, 'Before Christ', but there is a simple explanation. Numbering years from the beginning of the 'Christian Era' was only adopted by Christians in the 6th century, replacing a system of numbering years from the date of the foundation of Rome (A. U. C. – *Ab urbe condita*). Unfortunately, they made an arithmetical error which would place the birth of Jesus four years after the death of Herod the Great, in clear contradiction of Matthew's Gospel. It is easier now to think of the birth of Jesus as about 6BC than to alter all other dates by six years. The 20th century equivalents are given to indicate the time scale.

1st Century		20th Century
6BC	Birth of Jesus	1894
4BC	Death of King Herod the Great	1896
AD6	The boy Jesus in the Temple	1906
27	Baptism of Jesus and the start of his public ministry	1927
30	March: crucifixion, resurrection and ascension of Jesus	1930
	May: Pentecost; Holy Spirit comes to the apostles	
	The apostles of Jesus begin to arrange 'gospel' material about Jesus for their missionary work	

182

33	Martyrdom of Stephen; conversion of Paul	1933
45	Paul's first missionary journey (Asia Minor)	1945
48	Council of Jerusalem (Acts 15)	1948
49-52	Paul's second missionary journey	1949
	(Crete, Asia Minor and Greece)	
	Letters: 1 & 2 Thessalonians	
53-58	Paul's third missionary journey	1953
	(Asia Minor, Greece, Syria)	
	Letters: Philippians; 1 Corinthians	
	Galatians; 2 Corinthians	
	Romans; Philemon	
58	Paul arrested in the Temple in Jerusalem	1958
60	Paul goes to Rome for his legal appeal before the Emperor	
	Nero	1960
61-63	Paul under house arrest in Rome for his appeal	1961
	Letters: Colossians; Ephesians	
63-64	Paul freed; mission to Spain?	1963
	Letters: 1 Timothy; Titus	
	Letter: 1 Peter	
	MARK'S GOSPEL	
64	(Burning of Rome; local persecution of Christians)	1964
	Letter: 2 Peter	
	Peter martyred in Rome	
66-70	The Jewish War between Rome and the Palestinian Jews	1966
	Letters: 2 Timothy; Hebrews	
	Paul arrested again and martyred in Rome	
70	Destruction of Jerusalem by the Romans	1970
	Letter of James	
73	Rome captures Masada, the last Jewish stronghold	1973
75	**MATTHEW'S GOSPEL**	1975
	LUKE'S GOSPEL and **The Acts of the Apostles**	
91	**Letter of Jude**	1991
95	Persecution of Christians by Emperor Domitian	
	Book of Revelation	
96	Emperor Nerva; persecutions ease	1996
	Letters: 1, 2 & 3 John	
	JOHN'S GOSPEL	

End of the New Testament writings because all the apostles of Jesus have died and there is no one left who can authenticate anything written about him.

INDEX OF ARTISTS AND WORKS

185

Picture acknowledgements

Pictures courtesy of the Bridgeman Art Library, with the exception of:

E.T. Archive
pp 7, 8–9, 16, 18, 25, 29, 41, 53, 125, 131, 163

Painton Cowen
pp 23, 28, 100, 141

Sonia Halliday Photographs
pp 11, 13, 33, 45, 65, 83, 91, 95, 107, 111, 115, 127, 139, 152, 157, 179

Kunsthalle, Hamburg
89

Cover back and front, pp 43, 123, 148–9, 154 by kind permission of the National Gallery, London